REVELATION
as Civil Disobedience

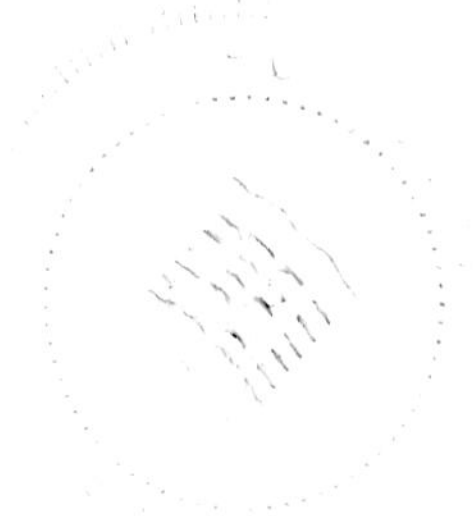

Thomas B. Slater

REVELATION

as CIVIL DISOBEDIENCE

Witnesses *Not* Warriors in John's Apocalypse

Nashville

REVELATION AS CIVIL DISOBEDIENCE:
Witnesses Not Warriors in John's Apocalypse

Library of Congress Control Number: 2019948259

ISBN: 978-1-5018-4174-3

19 20 21 22 23 24 25 26 27 28—10 9 8 7 6 5 4 3 2 1
MANUFACTURED IN THE UNITED STATES OF AMERICA

In memory of
William R. Farmer and George E. Howard

CONTENTS

ACKNOWLEDGMENTS

Many thanks to those institutions and persons who have helped me to make this publication possible. I am indebted to the editor of the Library of New Testament Studies (T&T Clark, 1999), who has graciously allowed me to use portions of my *Christ and Community*; to the editor of *Biblica* for allowing me to use my essay "Dating the Apocalypse to John (*Bib* 84 [2003]: 252–58); to the editor of *Review and Expositor* for allowing me to use my essays "Context, Christology and Civil Disobedience" (*RevExp* 106 [2009]: 51–56) and "Dating the Apocalypse to John, Revisited" (*RevExp* 114 [2017]: 247–53).

I am also very indebted to several individuals who have been instrumental in helping me to bring the work to fruition. My colleague Zinetta McDonald at the University of Georgia; Peter Rhea Jones and Denise Massey at McAfee School of Theology; David Cressman and Lynn Mims, friends since seminary at Perkins; Ben Rothwell, Loren Lasch, and Mariclair Partee, Episcopal priests who were my students at the University of Georgia, as well as Mark Chancey, who also studied with me at UGA; and Ca Trice Glenn, Taisha Seabolt, Sarah Murray, Priscilla Bryant, Natalie Vincent King, Man Kit (Joseph) Poon, Greg Paulson, Leah Robinson, Kris Aaron, and Harrison Litzell, my students at McAfee. At various points in the journey, each of these persons encouraged me to continue the journey and I am very grateful.

Without a doubt, the most influential persons in my professional journey have been Harold Attridge, my DMin supervisor at Perkins, the late Graham Stanton, my PhD supervisor at King's College London, the late William R. Farmer and the late George E. Howard. I have already dedicated earlier publications to Dr. Attridge and Dr. Stanton and I felt strongly that I must dedicate this work to my friends who meant so much to me. Dr. Farmer was my first New Testament Greek professor. After three weeks I wanted to drop the course, but he guilt-tripped me into staying. From that semester until his passing, he continuously supported my journey. He seemed to have a knack for giving good advice. For example, he helped in selecting a graduate program and also in selecting a publisher for my PhD thesis. When George Howard wrote him looking for someone to teach New Testament at the University of Georgia, Dr. Farmer suggested me. When I went up for tenure there, Dr. Farmer was one of my referees. George Howard was also an excellent mentor, helping me to navigate the tenure process, teaching me my role as a faculty member. These men believed in me. Unlike many Euro-Americans, they understood what it meant to be marginalized and reached out to help me. And that made all the difference. To work in the New Testament academy means to be marginalized if one is different. We are told that we are too subjective by people who are just as subjective. But their subjectivity passes as normal because it represents the majority view. Still we do our work because we are accustomed to struggle. This present work is part of the struggle. It is a presentation by a marginalized member of the New Testament academy. Saying this is not an excuse or apologetics. It is an affirmation of faith.

PREFACE

This study has its genesis in the last days of writing "Christ and Community," my PhD thesis at King's College London (supervised by the late Graham Stanton). While reading the thesis one final time, I realized defeating evil through faithfully witnessing (not through violence) was central to the christological and soteriological message of John's vision. I identified this as a form of civil disobedience. Since I was under some time constraints, I did not want to rewrite the thesis entirely. Rather, I went through the thesis and made insertions at key points. It was my intention to return to the topic at a later time.

Christian victory over evil came through suffering. This victory required an unwavering witness. As with Christ, it could lead to death. When this witness occurred before Roman officials or provincial leaders in service to the imperial cult, it became a form of civil disobedience. Thus, within this context, just as the slain Lamb has replaced the Lion of Judah, witnessing faithfully even unto death has replaced making war for the Apocalypse. These two transformations, from Lion to Lamb and from making war to bearing witness, will lead to a third transformation, the transformation of *marturia* from witnessing in court to witnessing fervently even if it means dying for one's beliefs.

The Christian community must remain spiritually strong throughout the end-time trials. This fact has escaped many contemporary Christians for two reasons. First and foremost, most North American and European Christians do not live under duress and constant pressure to conform and change their beliefs. They assume the biblical context is no different.

Second, many assume that they shall be raptured and escape these trials, as in the Gospels (e.g., Matt 24:36-44). There is no rapture in John's Apocalypse. Saint and sinner alike must endure the end-time trials. Indeed, the vision distinguishes strong beliefs and faith (e.g., 2:14-15; 3:1-3, 15-19). One may hold certain beliefs but acquiesce under pressure or be seduced away from them. True faith, however, informs, empowers, and sustains one's actions.

For many Christians, Revelation is a scary book. Thus, they avoid it. This is true of pastors and laypersons. Many pastors avoid Revelation because it is not as straightforward as the rest of the New Testament. It is loaded with symbolic references and coded messages, the narrative repeats itself, the images are often very old and seem foreign to contemporary Christians, and many scholars debate what certain things mean. The Revelation to John has the same problems we find throughout the New Testament, but within the symbolic universe of apocalyptic thinking they are more frequent and more mystifying. Coupled with the fact that this book depicts the end of time, interpreting Revelation is a mountain too high for some to climb.

The centrality of a faithful witness in Revelation has not gone unnoticed. Brian Blount, for example, has connected the centrality of a faithful witness to Revelation as resistance literature.[1] This present study goes a step further by arguing that the social setting, the Christology, and the centrality of witnessing are inseparable and explain one another in John's Apocalypse.

In 2003, I presented the Jackson Lecture at Perkins School of Theology: "Context, Christology and Civil Disobedience in John's Apocalypse." I also presented a similar paper at the 2006 International SBL meeting in Edinburgh, Scotland ("The Book of Revelation as Civil Disobedience") and published "Context, Christology and Civil Disobedience in John's Apocalypse" in *Review and Expositor* 106 (2009): 51–56. I am most appreciative of both the questions and the encouragement I encountered at Perkins and the SBL in Edinburgh that led to this publication.

1. Brian Blount, "Reading Revelation Today: Witness as Active Resistance," *Int* 54 (2000): 398–409.

This book addresses the Book of Revelation on two fronts. Those on the left decry the violence of the book while those on the right exploit the violence in it. Both assessments have missed the point that Revelation does not command or teach Christians to take up arms to defeat evil. Rather, following Christ, it encourages Christians to defeat evil through their faithful witness. For the Book of Revelation, God's dealing with unjust people is not pretty, but judgment is God's prerogative alone. God does not even share it with the "Left Behind Batallion," a fact missed (or ignored) by those on the left and those on the right. This type of polarization has become too common in American society. It is entrenched because both sides seek to advance their own agendas rather than allow Scripture to inform their faith and transform their behavior. It occurs when sophisticated eisegesis is mistaken for responsible exegesis. It occurs when methodology overcomes content and obscures the biblical context.

Moreover, some exegetes argue that there was no Christian suffering in Roman Asia, that John was a lone wolf who produced a work very different from the rest of the New Testament. This book will show that nothing could be further from the truth. Throughout the New Testament one encounters many examples of Christian suffering. John's Apocalypse expresses the same early Christian perspectives, themes, and practices, including harassment and suffering, as other books of the New Testament.

Finally, some Christians on the right believe that they are "under siege" by "liberal democracies." In actuality, they simply do not like criticism or losing influence. White law enforcement officials are not killing their unarmed children. They are not the last ones hired and the first ones fired. Board rooms have not suddenly become more racially diverse to the point that Caucasian men now constitute the minority in Fortune 500 companies, nor do they complain of racial profiling running rampant across the country. No one burns crosses in their yards or enters their churches to kill innocent persons. They simply do not enjoy the privilege of being white to the same degree as seventy years ago. Lack of privilege is their "cross" to bear, not lack of access to power. The Book of Revelation was not written for persons under this type of "siege." It was written for persons whose lives could be threatened because of their beliefs. It was written for people who refused to yield under immense social pressure. It was written for persons who were actually under siege, not for persons clinging disparately to their privileged status.

The Book of Revelation can be a very scary book. When teaching introductory courses on the New Testament, I tell students that I will explain the book to them in such a way that they can read the book after 10 p.m. and sleep peacefully. According to my students, I am reasonably successful in this regard. I hope the readers of this book will have the same experience. Sweet dreams!

—Thomas B. Slater
Lent 2019

ABBREVIATIONS

AB	Anchor Bible
ACNT	Augsburg Commentaries on the New Testament
AOT	H. F. D. Sparks, ed., *The Apocryphal Old Testament* (New York: Oxford University Press, 1984)
BECNT	Baker Exegetical Commentary on the New Testament
Bib	*Biblica*
GNS	Good News Studies
HDR	Harvard Dissertations in Religion
HNT	Handbuch zum Neuen Testament
ICC	International Critical Commentary
JSNTSup	*Journal for the Study of the New Testament Supplement Series*
NCBC	New Cambridge Bible Commentary
NIB	Leander Keck et al., eds., *The New Interpreter's Bible*, 12 vols. (Nashville: Abingdon Press, 1994–98).
NTL	New Testament Library

NTS	*New Testament Studies*
OTP	J. H. Charlesworth, ed., *Old Testament Pseudepigrapha*, 2 vols. (Peabody, MA: Hendrickson, 1983)
RevExp	*Review and Expositor*
SBLDS	Society of Biblical Literature Dissertation Series
SEG	Supplementum epigraphicum graecum
SNTSMS	Society for New Testament Studies Monograph Series
ST	*Studium*
TDNT	Gerhard Kittel and Gerhard Friedrich, eds., *Theological Dictionary of the New Testament*, trans. G. W. Bromiley, 10 vols. (Grand Rapids: Eerdmans, 1977)
THNTC	Two Horizons New Testament Commentary

Chapter 1

APOCALYPSE DEFINED

The genre of apocalypse gets its name from the opening line of the Book of Revelation: *apokalypsis*. This Greek word means "to reveal," thus the English title "Revelation." Biblical apocalyptic literature, however, did not begin with the Book of Revelation or the book of Daniel in the Old Testament. It has roots in the culture of the ancient Near East and clearly builds upon perceptions and images found in Ezekiel, Isaiah 40–55, and Zechariah.

Apocalypticism is a social movement borne from a social crisis. This crisis may have developed in one of two ways: (1) one group comes to power, or (2) one group totally dominates and exploits another. With the first situation, the displaced group retains some of its social status and political clout. And both groups may reverse roles sometime in the future. The less powerful group may be heavily influenced by apocalypticism but does not normally produce a full-blown apocalypse. The Jewish *Sibylline Oracles*, written by Jews living comfortably in Egypt, provide examples of such apocalyptic writings that are not apocalypses. A more recent example would be the 1994 Republican "Contract with America" during US President Bill Clinton's second term in office. These works envision a new social coalition but not the end of the social order.

The second type of crisis is more devastating. One group is totally superior in almost every way. The dominant group usually controls the economy, the political system, and the legal system. Members of the dominant group in the lowest socioeconomic class look down upon members of the subjugated group, regardless of their economic resources or intellectual gifts. The subjugated group has little to no status and little to no legal recourse. In such settings, oppressed persons often produce apocalypses that look to the future for divine deliverance.[1] The Revelation to John is such a book. Because John saw no other alternative within the social matrix to rectify the plight of Christians, he envisioned the end of the world that would reverse the status quo.

Thus, we distinguish between apocalyptic literature and an apocalypse. Apocalyptic literature refers to writings that have been influenced by apocalypticism and also display some of the features common to apocalypses but are not themselves representative of the genre. An apocalypse, on the other hand, is representative of the genre and also embodies most of the features common to it. Here is a definition from the Society of Biblical Genre Project, which has become a standard for many in New Testament studies:

> A genre of revelatory literature with a narrative framework, in which a revelation is mediated by an otherworldly being to a human recipient, disclosing a transcendent reality which is both temporal, insofar as it envisages eschatological salvation, and spatial insofar as it involves another supernatural world.[2]

This definition is specific enough to identify chief features found in the vast majority of works in this genre, yet flexible enough to allow for variations within it.

Features of an Apocalypse
• a vision mediated by an otherworldly figure, usually an angel
• a human seer who is a past (i.e., deceased) great worthy
• usually derives from a social crisis
• pseudepigraphical, written under a false name
• dualistic and deterministic
• hidden until the eve of the end time
• envisions a new world order

1. Some oppressed persons become "freedom fighters" in order to rectify what they deem as an unjust situation. The dominant group often refers to them as "terrorists." It depends very much on one's social location.

2. J. J. Collins, "Introduction: Towards the Morphology of a Genre," *Semeia* 14 (1979): 9. Too frequently modern genre critics allow rigid definitions that suit contemporary concerns and agendas but do not respect the originality of a given, nontechnical ancient writer to influence their conclusions. We should not hold John the Prophet to the same rigorous genre-critical standards that we might expect of Toni Morrison, Tom Clancy, or Danielle Steele.

An apocalypse is also a vision normally presented by divine messenger or an archangel to a (deceased) foundational figure in a particular religious tradition. The apocalypse gives the intended community a vision of a hopeful future that, in turn, gives the community strength during its present trials. The messenger being comes from the transcendent world and gives the vision a sense of inescapable finality. The human recipient is rarely the local shepherd down the road but usually a noted figure of the past, again giving the message a degree of authenticity. Thus the recipients are extremely open to the possibility that the visions, coming from a transcendent world and transmitted by a legendary figure, will lead to a transformation of the present social order: it will be a new, blessed world order where the saints will receive honor, be blessed, and be empowered.

In addition to the previous features, Jewish and Christian apocalypses during the Greco-Roman period displayed most of the following general characteristics:

First, they derived from a context of crisis where two groups opposed one another. One had more power than the other. The group not in power sees itself in a hopeless situation and looks to the heavens for deliverance.

Second, apocalypses usually were written under a false name of a deceased worthy. This feature is called pseudonymity and makes the book pseudepigraphical, a false writing.

Third, these books had an Us versus Them dualism. There was no middle ground. Everything was in black and white. This affirmed the faith of the community under duress and also confirmed the downfall of their opponents.

Fourth, often these visions were supposedly hidden and sealed until the end, when all their predictions would come true. In fact, most apocalypses contained a series of prophecies after the fact, what scholars called *ex eventu* prophecies. Since the earlier "prophecies" have been fulfilled, the readers may have confidence that all the visions will come true in the end.

Fifth, apocalypses often employed past traditions and infused them with new meaning, thus providing a link with the past that conveyed to the reader a vision of the future that gave comfort and strength in the present. The link with the past gave solace and encouragement to remain faithful in the midst of tribulation.

Finally, these works envisioned a new world order that completely replaces the present one. The cosmos is reborn completely and those who were out of favor become the favored ones, and vice versa.

While no single apocalypse has all these features, it will display a majority of them if it is to be classified as an apocalypse. In this way, each apocalypse manages to be unique while still incorporating characteristics and traditions common to a much wider circle. The Revelation to John is unique in that it was not written under a false name (though we do not know exactly who John of Patmos was) and was not hidden or sealed until the end (22:10). John writes in his own name and on his own authority. Moreover, the Messiah, not an angel, is the coauthor and giver of the apocalypse. These types of similarities and differences are characteristics of this genre and give Revelation its unique character.

Called through a Vision
Like John, Paul was called through a vision of Christ. (Gal 1:15-16; Rev 1:1-2, 9-20)

This John is apparently not John the apostle. John of Patmos never appeals to apostolic authority nor does he refer to the apostolic Twelve as though he belonged to the group. The apostolic office and apostolic authority were extremely important factors in the first Christian century. Apostles were seen as the most authoritative and most reliable witnesses (see 1 Cor 9:1-2). Nonetheless, he is an authority figure among the churches of Roman Asia and that in itself is sufficient for him to speak with authority.

Some would say that arguing against apostolic authorship undermines the canonical authority for the Book of Revelation. However, those who argue ardently for apostolic authorship tend to affirm a literal interpretation of Scripture. Nowhere in Revelation does the book seek apostolic authority. This is most notable in Revelation 2:2, where John questions the apostolic credentials of some of his opponents. If John were an apostle, this would have been the place to say so. More important, it is not who wrote the book that makes it Scripture but Who inspired the book. Throughout Christian history, many faithful believers have found the Book of Revelation inspiring, insightful, and revelatory.

Dating the Book

The date of authorship for Revelation is important for several reasons. A correct dating between 68–70 CE enables one to understand better the context and rationale for the Book of Revelation. Moreover, a correct dating enables one to see parallels with contemporary Christian and non-Christian writings. Finally, it enables us to obtain a more complete understanding of early Christianity. Indeed, various early Christian witnesses provide records of Christian suffering (e.g., Philippians, 1 Peter). While Christians responded differently to their plights, they shared a belief that not responding violently was the most appropriate Christian witness (Phil 1:27-30; Jas 1:4; 1 Pet 4:12-19; Rev 6:9-11). John's Apocalypse is an example of nonviolent civil disobedience and it gives us more data about nascent Christianity.

First, it provides another look into early Christianity within the movement's first decades. A few examples will suffice. Like the Gospel of John 1:1-3, Colossians 1:15-20, and Philippians 2:6, Revelation argues that Christ is a divine being with powers and roles previously reserved for God Almighty alone (e.g., 1:5; 5:12-14; 17:14). Like Ephesians 6:10-20, Revelation expresses in military terms the difficulty of a Christian lifestyle (19:11-21). Moreover, Revelation uses Christ's suffering as a means to understanding the plight of Christians in the first century (cf. Rev 5; Phil 3:17-21; 1 Pet 2:21-25). In these and other ways, Revelation is in step with other New Testament traditions and shows that certain beliefs were more widespread than previously believed.

Second, it also provides another side of some debates. For example, while 1 Peter called Christians to obey Roman authority (2:13), Revelation severely challenges Roman hegemony (chs. 13; 17–18). While Paul argued that eating meat offered to idols was permissible if it did not lead a brother or sister astray (1 Cor 8 and 10), John twice condemns such practices (Rev 2:14, 20). Why is this significant? How might our understanding of the Apostolic Council in Acts 15 (see Galatians 2) be different if we had access to Barnabas or Peter's perspectives? Revelation gives us more data for our study of nascent Christianity.

Finally, if Revelation is dated late in the first century, well after the destruction of the temple and the suppression of a Jewish revolt in 70 CE, some scholars imagine a pattern of widespread harassment and oppression against Gentile Christians that had spread deep in the empire, across Asia, where Christianity spread and multiplied rapidly during the last quarter of the first century. However, if the imagination that produced the Apocalypse took shape before the destruction of the Jerusalem temple, early Jewish Christianity was more localized and coping with laxity or apathy. They were also asking what adjustments they might make in their behavior and practices.

Some might rightly ask just what difference it makes when this book came together. It is important for two reasons. An earlier dating explains why the book is so Jewish. It is both Christian and Jewish at a point in time when Christianity was still a Jewish movement. Also, clarity on the dating of Revelation gives us additional insight into early Christian history. Specifically, we see aspects of the other side of key early Christian debates.[3]

Well-intentioned people often disagree on dates while others could not care less. The reality of an early composition date will create challenges for some Christians in both the academy and the parish. There is a clear bias toward a Pauline sensibility in both worlds. Academic settings, often heavily influenced by The Reformation and neo-orthodoxy in the twentieth century, find much in Paul that reaffirms their basic theological convictions. The parish setting sees in Paul's writings themes that inspire and nourish faith (e.g., kosher free religion, beautiful prose [1 Cor 13, and so forth]). These things are truly positives. On the other hand, from my days as a parish minister I was constantly reminded that well-intentioned people often disagree intensely. Fortunately as well, God's grace covered us

3. I am indebted to Denise Massey, associate professor of pastoral care, McAfee School of Theology, Mercer University, in private discussion for this final insight.

all. No one has exclusive rights to the complete truth. People in the biblical narrative were no less human than we are and no less in need of grace.

Internal factors within the text itself strongly indicate that the Book of Revelation was written between 68–70 CE. The majority opinion among biblical scholars is that Revelation was written later during Emperor Domitian's reign (81–96 CE). However, this date is based entirely upon the external witness of Irenaeus in *Against Heresies* 5, a century after Domitian. Supporters of a late first-century date look for internal evidence that fits with the reign of Domitian. Some others notice textual references to "Babylon" in support of a later date but overlook the still-standing Jerusalem temple described in John's apocalypse.

Some exegetes and interpreters have argued that the Domitianic date is correct because it coincides with Domitian's claim to divine honors, putting pressure on Christians to worship the emperor as a divine being. And other scholars have stressed that "Babylon" became a code name for Rome near the end of the first Christian century, as evidenced in 1 Peter 5:13; 2 Esdras 3:1; *Sibylline Oracles* 5, 143, and 159; and 2 Baruch 10:1-3, 11:1, and 67:7, all dated between 60 and 120 CE. Many commentators note that several of these passages refer to Rome/Babylon as the second destroyer of Jerusalem and the second temple in 70 CE.[4] Here Leonard Thompson speaks for many: "In Jewish literature, the enemy Rome is designated Edom, Kittim, and Egypt, as well as Babylon. For the most part, however, the identity with Babylon occurs after 70 CE, that is, Rome is called Babylon after it destroys Jerusalem and the Temple."[5]

Still others have argued that the Nero myth in Revelation 13:1-4, 18 and 17:9-11, which symbolically represents the first Roman emperors, would indicate that the Domitianic date is most probably correct, that Domitian is the second Nero, the eighth ruler. Revelation 17:9-11 reads as follows:

4. On dates for these books, see *OTP* 1:390, 520, 615–17; D. Balch, *Let Wives Be Submissive*, SBLDS 26 (Chico, CA: Scholars Press, 1981), 137–38; J. H. Elliott, *A Home for the Homeless* (Philadelphia: Fortress, 1981), 78–84. See also G. A. Krodel, *Revelation*, ACNT (Minneapolis: Augsburg Fortress, 1989), 63; M. E. Boring, *Revelation*, Interpretation (Louisville: Westminster John Knox, 1989), 10–12.

5. L. Thompson, *The Book of Revelation: Apocalypse and Empire* (Oxford: Oxford University Press, 1990), 14. See also B. K. Blount, *Revelation: A Commentary*, NTL (Louisville: Westminster John Knox, 2009), 8.

> Here is the mind that has wisdom: The seven heads are seven mountains upon which the woman sits. They are also seven kings. Five have fallen, one is, another has yet to appear, and whenever he appears it is necessary for him to remain a brief time. And the beast who was and is not, he is the eighth and is from the seven and he goes to perdition. (author translation)

Proponents of the Domitianic date, whether they begin counting with Julius Caesar, or with Augustus Caesar, or Caligula, the emperor who first openly demanded divine honors, find a way to end with Domitian, omitting Galba, Otho, and Vitellius, who each ruled briefly from 68 to 69, between Nero and Vespasian.[6]

Emperors of the Roman Empire from 31 BCE to 138 CE	
Caesar Augustus (Octavian)	31 BCE–14 CE
Tiberius	14–37 CE
Gaius (Caligula)	37–41 CE
Claudius	41–54 CE
Nero	54–68 CE
Galba	68–69 CE
Otho	69 CE
Vitellius	69 CE
Vespasian	69–79 CE
Titus	79–81 CE
Domitian	81–96 CE
Nerva	96–98 CE
Trajan	98–117 CE
Hadrian	117–138 CE

The Domitianic date is really based upon Irenaeus, a distant witness at least a century later, who has not proven a reliable witness. Irenaeus is far removed from the actual events and at best must rely upon second-hand witnesses himself. Thompson (and others) has demonstrated clearly

6. See R. H. Charles, *A Critical and Exegetical Commentary on the Revelation of St. John*, ICC, 2 vols. (New York: Scribner's, 1920),1.xci–xcvii; 2:68–70; J. H. Ulrichsen, "Die sieben Haupter und die zehn Horner. Zur Datierung der Offenbarung des Johannes," *ST* 39 (1985): 1–20; Krodel, *Revelation*, 297.

that there was no empire-wide persecution of Christians inaugurated by Domitian.[7] Moreover, Thompson has shown conclusively that the writings of the Roman historians who were Irenaeus's primary sources had intentionally given a poor depiction of Domitian in order to ingratiate themselves to Trajan and his new imperial family. Thus, for these reasons, Irenaeus is not the most reliable source for dating the Apocalypse to John and can only be used as a supporting witness.[8]

While some have argued that there was great pressure upon Christians to conform to regional religio-political expectations during Domitian's reign,[9] in actuality those pressures were present from the early days of the empire in the Roman province of Asia. Dio Cassius notes that divine honors to the imperial family began during Caesar Augustus's reign.[10] Simon Price also provides solid evidence of heavy competition among the cities of the province to be designated as *neokoros*, an official site of the imperial cult.[11] This status brought political, economic, and other social benefits to cities and regions. Commercial building projects, cultural enterprises, and relief after natural disasters were some of the benefactions that came to these cities. Additionally, these localities forged personal bonds with the imperial family, which provided additional social benefits for cities and their leaders. Similarly, Price, Friesen, Rowland, and others argue that those who resisted conformity to regional traditions and pressures would have faced local abuse, discrimination, and other forms of social harassment and might well have produced protest literature as a way of dealing with social stresses at any time during the first half-century of the Roman Empire.

7. See, for example, Thompson, *Revelation*, 95–115.

8. I have discussed this in more detail in Thomas B. Slater, *Christ and Community: A Socio-Historical Study of the Christology of Revelation*, JSNTSup (Sheffield, UK: Sheffield Academic, 1999), 26–42.

9. For example, Boring, *Revelation*, 8–25.

10. *Roman Histories* 51.20.6–7. See also SEG 23.206.

11. Simon Price, *Rituals and Power: The Roman Imperial Cult in Asia Minor* (Cambridge: Cambridge University Press, 1984), 24–25, 249–74.

Additionally, from a non-Christian perspective, refusal by some to not participate in the imperial cult (the worship of the emperor) might bring the wrath of the gods who placed the imperial family on the throne.[12]

> Other cults might be useful in municipal religion, in household cults, in group activity, or in combinations thereof. Only imperial cults could operate in all of these spheres while providing a cultic expression for the empire. . . . The emperors, their families, the Senate, and the city of Rome had redefined the structure of life in the Mediterranean world. Worship of them could be woven into all levels of the provincial experience . . . as the preeminent expression of the dominant imperial discourse.[13]

Babylon is indeed used as a code name for Rome in the latter decades of the first century CE and the early decades of the second century CE in 1 Peter, *Sibylline Oracle* 5, 2 Esdras, and 2 Baruch. However, both Daniel and *Sibylline Oracle* 3.300–309 use Babylon as a code name for Syria in the second century BCE, though the Syrians did not destroy the temple. Both books use Babylon as a way to refer to an evil empire, and many have shown in detail Revelation's debt to Daniel.[14]

"Babylon" in Daniel 7 and Sibylline Oracle 3

In the first year of Babylon's King Belshazzar, Daniel had a dream—a vision in his head as he lay on his bed. (Dan 7:1)

God prompted me to say this first, how many grievous woes the Immortal devised for Babylon, because it destroyed his great Temple. (Sib. Or. 3)[15]

Observe that the temple is still standing in the visionary action of Revelation 11:1-2.[16] Indeed, New Testament scholars consistently date books

12. See C. Rowland, *The Open Heaven* (New York: Crossroad, 1982), 412. See also S. J. Friesen, *Imperial Cults and the Apocalypse to John* (Oxford: Oxford University Press, 2001), 23–131. Similarly, after September 11, 2001, some conservative Christian leaders said the attacks resulted from the sins of American society.

13. Friesen, *Imperial Cults and the Apocalypse*, 126–27.

14. For example, G. K. Beale, *John's Use of the Old Testament in Revelation*, JSNTSup 166 (Sheffield, UK: Sheffield Academic, 1998).

15. J. J. Collins, trans., "Sibylline Oracles," *OTP*, vol. 1.

16. R. J. Bauckham's interpretation of Revelation 8:1 supports my point that the temple is still standing when John writes. Bauckham convincingly argues that the thirty-minute silence in heaven parallels

based upon whether or not there is a reference to the destruction of the temple. The Romans destroyed the temple in 70 CE. If there is no reference to its destruction (cf. Mark 13:2), and it is still standing in a given work, scholars date the work prior to 70. If it is not standing, scholars date the work after 70. In Revelation we read, "Then I was given a measuring rod, which was like a pole. And I was told, 'Get up and measure God's temple, the altar, and those who worship there" (Rev 11:1). To be sure, this is visionary rhetoric, yet it presumes the existence of the Jerusalem temple.

More important for dating purposes, John's Apocalypse uses Babylon to represent the political presence of Satan in the world in Revelation 12:1–13:18 and 17:1–19:4: Babylon is the enemy of God that must be punished in the end times. The writer of Revelation is reading Daniel and reapplying the meaning of Babylon. And Jewish apocalypses regularly adapted and transformed traditional materials for their own times: for example, Davidic messianic expectation (Rev 5:4-12; cf. 2 Esd 11:36-46), the one like a human being (or son of man: cf. Dan 7:13 and Rev 1:7-16), and the Leviathan-Behemoth myth (Rev 13:1-18; cf. 2 Esd 6:49) are each reinterpreted in John's Apocalypse.

Two Beasts

Then you kept two living creatures in reserve; you named one Behemoth and the other Leviathan. (2 Esd 6:49, author translation)

The symbolic references to the emperor found in Revelation 13 and 17 are also important internal witnesses that help date this book. Too many exegetes have omitted Galba, Otho, and Vitellius from their lists without proving that John would have also omitted them, working backward from Domitian in order to make the presupposed dating fit the data instead of reverse. After Nero's death in 68 CE, Galba, Otho, and Vitellius all ruled briefly as emperor until Vespasian eventually took control in 69 CE. Others have all shown that ancient writings—including *Sibylline*

the burning of incense each morning in the temple after the lamb had been sacrificed. This lasted approximately thirty minutes (*The Climax of Prophecy: Studies in the Book of Revelation* [Edinburgh: T&T Clark, 1993], 70–83); see also Wilson, "Domitianic Date," 599–605.

Oracle 5 and Roman writers such as Suetonius, Tacitus, and Eutropius—included these three men in their respective lists of emperors.[17] For dating purposes, internal evidence would compel readers to take into account that the temple still stands and the emperors Galba, Otho, and Vitellius should be counted when considering the date for John's Apocalypse.

Bell avoids counting the Roman emperors by beginning with either Julius Caesar or Augustus Caesar. Instead, he begins with the fifth emperor who is clearly Nero (see Rev 13:3 and 17:9-11). He notes that Roman writers Suetonius, Plutarch, and Eutropius included Galba, Otho, and Vitellius. Additionally, he correctly argues that for 2 Esdras 12:16 (dated ca. 100 CE) to speak of twelve emperors, it must include Galba, Otho, and Vitellius. According to Roman custom, anyone duly inducted into an office would have been included in any official list of office holders. Bell dates the Apocalypse between June 68 and January 69 during Galba's reign.[18] "Armies in Spain, Germany and Judaea are supporting rival candidates for the principate. Where there had been order and peace, for as long as any man living could recall, there is suddenly anarchy and civil war."[19] Finally, he notes that while Suetonius mentions Nero's persecution, he does not mention one initiated by Domitian.[20] This political unrest throughout the Roman Empire between 68 and 70 CE would have seemed like the end of the world to many people, Christian and non-Christian, after a century of Pax Romana (the peace of Rome).

Concurring with Bell, Rowland also includes Galba, Otho, and Vitellius when reading Revelation 13 and 17. He agrees with Bell that Nero is clearly the fifth emperor and that the book was written during the reign of Galba. "No other explanation of these verses matches the simplicity of this interpretation, which, one may assume, would also have been the most obvious to the original readers of the document."[21] He adds again, concurring with Bell, that the political turmoil that ensued throughout

17. A. A. Bell Jr., "The Date of John's Apocalypse: The Evidence of Some Roman Historians Reconsidered," *NTS* 25 (1978): 93–102; Rowland, *Open Heaven*; Wilson, "Domitianic Date," 597–605.

18. Bell, "The Date," 97–102.

19. Bell, "The Date," 102.

20. Bell, "The Date," 96.

21. Rowland, "Open Heaven," 405.

the Roman Empire after Nero's death, during 68 CE, coupled with the apocalyptic imagery found in the book, clearly points to that year as the time of the writing of the Apocalypse of John.

Wilson emphasizes internal evidence, and he also includes Galba, Otho, and Vitellius in reckoning the list of emperors. He concurs with Bell and Rowland that Nero is clearly the fifth emperor. Wilson identifies 666 (Rev 13:18) as code for *NERON KAISAR*. "When the name is put into Hebrew and the numerical equivalents of the Hebrew letters are added together, the sum is 666." In addition, he provides the most credible explanation for the 616 variant reading in some manuscripts. "The 616 (variant) would take the final *nun* off the name Neron in order to render it Nero, the acceptable way of saying the name in Greek."[22] Since Nero is the fifth emperor, Galba is the sixth, "the one who is," and Otho is yet to come. For Wilson, as with Bell and Rowland, the Apocalypse was written during the reign of Galba. While I agree in general, elsewhere I have argued that John wrote Revelation during the reign of Vitellius, but the consequences for clear interpretation of the purpose for the work would hold if it were written during Galba's reign.[23]

I am, therefore, in general agreement with a date between 68 and 70 CE and would add three additional internal evidences. First are two examples found in Revelation 2:9 ("those who say they are Jews [though they are not, but are really Satan's synagogue])" and in 3:9 ("who say they are Jews and really aren't"), that have been overlooked. In both passages, being Jewish is the religious ideal. John did not criticize his opponents because they were Jews but because *they were not faithful Jews*. In the 60s CE Christianity was still very much a movement within Judaism. By the 90s Christianity was predominantly Gentile and many Christians either had been expelled from the synagogue or had left on their own and saw themselves separate from Judaism. A self-understanding as Jewish is more conceivable among Christians in the 60s than the 90s.

22. Wilson, "Domitianic Date," 598. This is an important contribution, for at once Wilson explains the variant and what the original reading would have been. Furthermore, he clearly demonstrates how more than one group would have understood the gematria to refer to Nero, even those who wanted to change the spelling.

23. T. B. Slater, "Dating the Apocalypse of John," *Bib* 84 (2003): 252–58; see also my "Dating the Apocalypse to John, Revisited," *RevExp* 114 (2018): 247–53.

A second factor overlooked in dating the book is John's position against eating meat offered to idols in Revelation 2:14 and 2:20, a position diametrically opposed to Paul's more moderate position in 1 Corinthians 8. John sees Paul's position as an unfaithful accommodation, if not capitulation, to social norms and expectations. It is highly *unlikely* that a Christian leader would openly oppose Paul during the 90s in the same general area where Paul had an extensive ministry and where Paul's letters would have been regularly quoted by Christians as authoritative. Indeed, virtually everyone in the 90s wants to be the acknowledged successor to Paul the apostle, as one who faithfully continues the Pauline tradition. However, we know from Paul's own letters of his ardent opponents in the 50s and 60s (e.g., Gal 1:10–2:10; 2 Cor 11:1-33). Opposition to Paul was real in the 60s, not so much in the 90s.

Concurrently, a third internal factor is the accusation of false apostles in Revelation 2:2: "You have tested those who say they are apostles but are not, and you have found them to be liars." Paul faced similar opposition in the 50s and 60s: "Am I not an apostle? Haven't I seen Jesus our Lord? . . . If I'm not an apostle to others, at least I am to you! You are the seal that shows I'm an apostle" (1 Cor 9:1-2).

By the 90s CE there was no longer any debate about who the apostles were. Rather, the argument was who faithfully followed the teachings and practices of the apostles. Such an assertion about false apostles would be much more likely during the 60s.[24] Paul faced stiff opposition in his lifetime about whether or not he was an apostle, but we have no record of such debates in the 90s.

Apostles in the New Testament

Some believed that only persons who followed Jesus before Easter could be an apostle (see Acts 1:15-26), while others believed the apostolic office denoted persons called by Jesus and who displayed extraordinary gifts (see Romans 16:7; Galatians 1:1). After the circulation of Paul's letters, this debate became moot.

24. Of course, twenty-first-century American Christianity is full of "apostles."

In sum, several internal factors indicate that Revelation was written between 68 and 70 CE. Again, first, one should include Galba, Otho, and Vitellius in a list of Roman emperors, as did other Roman writers. Second, the temple, destroyed in 70 CE, is depicted as still standing in Revelation 11. Third, the self-identification of Christians as Jews indicates an earlier rather than a later date in the first century. Fourth, it is more likely that a writer would take a theological position in contrast to Paul in the 60s CE rather than the 90s. Finally, it is also much more likely that there would be a discussion of who was a true apostle in the 60s than the 90s. In the 90s, discussion circulated around who was faithfully carrying on apostolic traditions, not who was or was not an apostle (e.g., *1 Clem.* 5, 42, and 45).[25] For these reasons, I believe that the best guess for when John recorded the Book of Revelation is somewhere between 68 and 70 CE.

The Social Context: Under Pressure

Contemporary biblical commentators have begun to question the traditional view that the Book of Revelation comes from a crisis situation. Some argue that there is no historical evidence to substantiate an empire-wide, official persecution of Christians during Domitian's reign.[26] Moreover, the absence of any mention of an empire-wide persecution of Christians in the letters/messages/oracles to the seven churches (Rev 2:1–3:22) indicates that the Book of Revelation was not written as a response to Christian suffering but as a response to various forms of religious laxity within these congregations, so they say. Finally, some argue that the Jewish and Christian communities had achieved a degree of socioeconomic status that removed any prejudices against them. The following section reexamines the debate in light of the extant Roman and Christian writings pertinent to the subject, demonstrating that there is no evidence showing

25. Further examples would include the many quotations and allusions to writings attributed to apostles throughout the Apostolic Fathers (see Ign. *Eph.* 18 and 20; Pol. *Phil.* 3–4; Did. 1.2–2.7; 4.1-8).

26. From my perspective, the Domitianic dating makes this argument moot. Moreover, the absence of a worldwide persecution does not negate a regional repression. While legal racial discrimination did not exist across the United States after the Civil War, it was legal in a given region of the country. At this same time, Catholics, Jews, and African Americans encountered bigotry throughout the country.

that Christians were held in high esteem. This section also demonstrates that many have misread the messages in Revelation 2–3 in ways that reveal their theological bias *against* the relevance of John's Apocalypse.

Students of the New Testament often have no idea what it means for a targeted community to live with unwarranted bigotry and prejudice. They speak and write as if Philo of Alexandria—a well-educated, wealthy, first-century Jewish philosopher—never made an appeal to the Roman emperor for relief from bigotry or as if he never wrote to defend and explain Judaism to the wider Roman society. They also often talk about Scripture as if Luke–Acts is not an example of a Christian writer defending and explaining Christianity to the Roman world. But the biblical writers did not do their work in a vacuum. They responded to social pressure.

Bigotry causes communities to make social adjustments to ease social pressures. In societies where the lion's share of power, wealth, and esteem accrue to a dominant class, "we" dress, express ourselves, and dream like "them" so that "they" might accept "us." It is not a stretch to say that we have accommodated ourselves to our environment. And in the process, we lose something of ourselves. When the dominant culture does not accept us, we hear a voice in the wilderness of our social despair telling us to be proud of who we *really* are and not to compromise. John is that voice speaking to seven churches in Roman Asia in 68–70 CE. John finds himself in such a place.

Be True to You!

James Brown sang, "Say it loud! I'm black and I'm proud!" Brown's lyric struck a chord in the African American community in the 1960s. Many African Americans found that their attempts were unsuccessful when trying to show the dominant culture that they too were as American as the WASP culture. Moreover, many African Americans felt that they had lost something of themselves in the attempt. As a result, many decided to be themselves, and others would simply have to make adjustments. Similarly, John tells Asian Christians, "Be true to you!"

Some have also pointed to the letters to the churches in Revelation 2–3[27] as proof that Revelation is not responding to a crisis of any type, arguing that the messages do not mention persecution or oppression but complacency, compromise, and accommodation as the chief problems for the churches in Asia.[28] These commentators have assumed (without proving) that since the messages are in prose they represent a more straightforward version of the apocalyptic visions. This is a natural assumption, but it is incorrect and has led to two misreadings. The first misreading relates to the general purpose of the letters; the second, to their interpretation.[29] Moreover, it demonstrates a lack of understanding how prejudice works and how people respond to it.

C. H. H. Scobie demonstrated that there is insufficient data in the messages to ascertain any substantial information about the broader society. Rather, they are "Christian prophetic oracles" that tell us much about John's relationship to these churches but little about the churches' relationship to the wider Roman Asian society.[30] I agree completely. The general function of Revelation 2–3 is to describe the internal religious life of each church so that each congregation might become spiritually strong enough to endure the coming apocalyptic trials and subsequently "enter the new Jerusalem."[31] Therefore, to expect Revelation 2–3 to provide us

27. I am aware of the form-critical debate in some circles concerning Revelation 2–3 as to whether or not these are true letters. I believe the conclusions reached thus far are partially correct. They are oracular in nature, as one might expect in an apocalyptic work, however, no other known apocalypse has anything like them. I think Paul's letter writing to Christians in the same region has influenced John to the point that he gives his vision these epistolary features. In this study, I refer to Revelation 2–3 as "messages," "letters" and "oracles" interchangeably since it is unlikely that John would have made such a fine distinction. Indeed, one of my critics on this topic, David Aune, has written, "The letter was one of the more flexible of ancient literary forms. Almost any kind of written text could be framed by formal epistolary features and regarded as a letter" ("The Bible and the Literature of Antiquity: The Greco-Roman Period," in *Harper's Bible Commentary*, ed. J. E. Mays et. al. [New York: Harper San Francisco, 1988], 48). When I refer to Revelation 2–3 as letters, I am saying no more than this.

28. E.g., J. P. M. Sweet, *Revelation* (London: SCM, 1979), 26–27; Richard Bauckham, *The Theology of the Book of Revelation* (New York: Cambridge University Press, 1993), 12–17. See also F. J. Murphy, *Fallen Is Babylon: The Revelation to John* (Harrisburg, PA: Trinity, 1998), 5–17.

29. This misreading of Revelation 2–3 occurs regardless of whether one refers to these missives as "letters," "oracles," or "messages."

30. C. H. H. Scobie, "Local References in the Letters to the Seven Churches," *NTS* 39 (1993): 606–24. Cf. D. E. Aune, "The Form and Function of the Proclamation to the Seven Churches (Revelation 2–3)," *NTS* 36 (1990): 182–204.

31. Cf. Bauckham, *Theology*, 14.

with some information about the relationship of the Christian community to its wider social context means asking questions these messages were never intended to answer. Only one message (Rev 2:8-11) discusses the relationship between Christians and non-Christians in Roman Asia in any detail. This is the first misreading.

The second misreading is more alarming. When one finds references to the wider social context in these messages, they describe Christian suffering. Therefore, it is not that suffering is not there, but that it has been overlooked to subversively undermine the Book of Revelation. The Book of Revelation has been exploited and often misread by persons on the Christian right who emphasize predicting the end or relating biblical prophecy to politics in the Middle East. Christians on the left have all too often responded to this by attacking or ignoring Revelation without asking if there might be another, more appropriate interpretation. For example, scholars on the left frequently say that Jesus's love ethic is not found in Revelation and that the book is too violent without noting that Christians are never encouraged to take arms but to witness faithfully instead. God alone judges in John's Apocalypse.

Revelation 2–3 has three clear examples of Christian suffering. In the letter to Smyrna (2:8-11) one finds mention of slander, religious infidelity, suffering, and impending imprisonment. There are tensions arising from both more traditional Jews and traditional Asian residents. Both would have wanted Christians to conform and become more traditional. The Jews probably wanted Christians to keep the Torah, stop referring to a convicted criminal (from their perspective) as the Messiah, and not refer to him as the divine Son of God. Pagans would have wanted Christians to participate in the imperial cult. Blount writes, "Smyrna was a hotbed of imperial cultic worship," and "Greco-Roman culture did not separate the sacred and secular realms, spiritual activity had dramatic political implications.[32] "Clearly, the faithfulness called for could very well entail a witness that results in the death of some of those in the church at Smyrna," and

32. Blount, *Revelation*, 53–54. Similarly, John Christopher Thomas and Frank D. Macchia, *Revelation*, THNTC (Grand Rapids: Eerdmans, 2016), 94–96. Determining which group is the genuine representative of Judaism is a key aspect, if not the key aspect, of this debate.

the readers would be encouraged by the fact that this exhortation "comes from 'the one who was dead and came to life' (Rev 2:8)."[33]

Moreover, the message to Pergamum goes to a church "where Satan's throne is" (Rev 2:13). This refers to the imperial cult. In John's Apocalypse, the emperor was Satan's agent. Pergamum had many pagan temples and the social influence of these temples and their religious traditions was extensive.[34] Revelation 2:13 also refers to the martyrdom of Antipas, "my faithful witness." And Thomas and Macchia remind readers that "in this verse Antipas, 'my faithful witness,' stands in extremely close solidarity with Jesus, 'the faithful witness.'"[35] Rather than see Antipas as the only martyr, Antipas is the symbol for what faithfulness requires for every Christian in Pergamum. Antipas provides a model for Christians under duress to emulate.[36] And for Blount, "Antipas is the ultimate representative of non-violent resistance."[37]

Revelation 3:8-10 refer to pressures upon Christians to conform to a more traditional form of Judaism (in the letter/message to Philadelphia). Although Christians in Philadelphia have little social capital, they have remained faithful and have not denied that they are Christians. This soundly implies that some have denied the name. This is a conflict within Judaism between Christians who affirm Jesus is the Jewish Messiah (and likely assert Jesus's divinity) and more traditional Jews who say Jesus is not the Messiah and is not divine.[38] Because of their faithfulness, Christ promises to protect them in the coming trials. Blount makes this clear: "Here, as in the Gospel, persecution is something that believers will endure (2:10). Their witness matters... because they give it in the circumstances of such duress, just as Christ himself did on the cross."[39] Likewise, Thomas and Macchia underscore this point: "Primarily, the hearers are to continue

33. Thomas and Macchia, *Revelation*, 97.

34. E. Lohmeyer, *Die Offenbarung des Johannes*, 2nd ed., HNT, 16 (Tubingen: J. C. B. Mohr, 1953), 24–25.

35. Thomas and Macchia, *Revelation*, 100.

36. Thomas and Macchia, *Revelation*, 100.

37. Blount, *Revelation*, 58.

38. For a more traditional Jewish messianic expectation, see 2 Esd 13.

39. Blount, *Revelation*, 77.

holding on to what they have, keeping Jesus's word of patient endurance and not denying his name, even in the face of persecution."[40] Again, it is not that the oracles do not mention Christian suffering; it is just overlooked.

Along with these two misreadings of Revelation is a lack of experience with how prejudice works. Often where there is strong prejudice, it can remain unseen for long periods of time to those directly unaffected by it. Experiences of hope and hopelessness frequently coexist in a society. In many instances, prejudices lie dormant until the dominant group feels threatened or when an opportunity arises for the majority group to openly express its true feelings. Those holding to a logic of prejudice believe that certain persons are less than human and can never equal the intelligence, talent, culture, or patriotism of those in the dominant social group. And people in the dominant group are usually resistant to change even in the face of extraordinary evidence to the contrary.[41] A few contemporary examples demonstrate the point. Between 1865 and 1900, many (if not most) nonblack Americans viewed black Americans as inferior, even if they felt slavery was wrong. In the twentieth century, many well-educated, middle-class black Americans sought to counter this impression by encouraging young black Americans to attend college, take up respected professions, and demonstrate that black Americans are not less than human. Four persons exemplified this vision: Percy L. Julian Sr., Marion Anderson, Ralph Bunche, and Benjamin Davis Sr.[42]

Percy Julian was an outstanding chemist who received a PhD at the University of Vienna. Julian was denied entrance into Harvard's PhD program because of his race. He was a pioneer in synthesizing drugs from plants, including testosterone. His work laid the foundation for the development of cortisone and corticosteroids. He held over one hundred chemical patents. Marian Anderson was one of the premier contraltos of

40. Thomas and Macchia, *Revelation*, 126; see also 118–26.

41. As an example of racism, police in Jefferson, Missouri, joked that Barack Obama would not serve out his first term because no black man ever held a job for four years.

42. These are representative not exhaustive figures. I intentionally omitted persons in popular culture such as Ella Fitzgerald, Dorothy Dandridge, Zora Neale Hurston, Jackie Robinson, and Joe Louis. African Americans are more than entertainers and professional athletes.

the twentieth century. She sang in every major venue in America and won international acclaim. The Daughters of the American Revolution stopped her from singing at Constitution Hall in 1939 because of her race. Ralph Bunche was one of the pioneers in the creation of the United Nations and won the Nobel Peace Prize for negotiating the first peace treaty between Israel and its Arab neighbors. And Benjamin Davis Sr. was the first black American promoted to the rank of general in the armed forces. He served honorably in World Wars I and II. All four received international acclaim and respect before the Montgomery bus boycott and the integration of Central High School in Little Rock in the 1950s. Outstanding contributions by black Americans across American society between 1900 and 1950 did not abate the undercurrent of racism in America and the need for the civil rights movement in the 1950s and 1960s.

I met several South Africans during the height of apartheid. I met black, colored, and Afrikaner South Africans who were outspoken opponents of apartheid. What surprised me was meeting wealthy black South Africans in the 1970s, persons whose standard of living far exceeded mine. Somehow in the midst of horrific circumstances they prospered, but they rightly understood that their prosperity was the exception to the rule.

Barack Obama served as president of the United States for eight years. And during his presidency, the Black Lives Matter movement emerged and has since gained a national following that includes persons across ethnic communities who are protesting the repeated shootings of unarmed black men across the country. As I write, some professional athletes refuse to stand for the national anthem because of these shootings.[43] As I write, minority and majority scholars in social science departments across the country decry the lack of diversity in many faculties simply because their colleagues have not tried to make such changes. As I write, many mainstream denominations that support liberal ideas are less likely to have a high percentage of integrated congregations or seek pastors without considering their ethnicity. All this is occurring in a country that twice elected

43. Standing for the national anthem is not a show of respect for the military, but a show of respect for the core values that all 300 million Americans hold dear. That is why it is the *national* anthem and not the *military* anthem. Some persons are not standing for the anthem because they believe that everyone does not share the values for which the anthem is but a symbol.

a black man to the highest office in the land. Signs of hope and signs of despair often coexist in the same society because bigotry has a long shelf life. Life is rarely black and white and even when it is, it is usually checkered. To assume that hope completely displaces despair, or vice versa, for John's context (and ours) says more about the social location of the interpreter than the subject under study.

The Revelation to John requires a similar nuanced and culturally informed reading. Hope and despair walked side by side for some Christians in Roman Asia. Religious laxity in John's Apocalypse does not reflect complete acceptance of Christians by the wider society but at best a degree of acceptance and attempts by some Christians to gain approval from their pagan peers. In fact, the argument that religious laxity alone was the reason for John's complaints without any outside pressure rings hollow because it fails to rightly understand accommodation as a response to pressure to conform. Prejudice is deep, embedded, and assumed. Prejudice is not always on display; it is frequently invisible. It often lies dormant until it can seize an opportunity to act or until it feels threatened. It is difficult for persons who are not prejudiced—especially those who have not experienced the exclusionary and diminishing power of prejudice—to perceive this impact.

Civil War in the 1990s in the Former Yugoslavia (Now Slovenia)

When I taught at the University of Georgia, one of my Muslim students from present-day Slovenia (the former Yugoslavia) told me that before the conflict in the Balkans with various ethnic groups seeking independence, Croats, Bosnian Muslims, Albanians, and Serbs had lived together without significant political violence since the end of World War II. When the totalitarian ruler Chairman Tito died in 1980, the old rivalries and tensions resurfaced with even greater potency, each group seeking more autonomy within Yugoslavia.

Accommodation sometimes reflects the loss of zeal by succeeding generations, but that usually coincides with a general acceptance of a group or movement. Such was not the case for Jewish Christians in the early days of the Roman Empire. We have two examples, one from the emperor Nero and another from Pliny, a provincial Roman governor. Nero convinced the citizens of Rome that Christians were to blame for the burning of the city without producing any evidence to substantiate his claim. Christians were publicly executed without trials. Similarly, Pliny tortured and killed Christians, believing that they were inherently evil. When he learned that they were not, he showed no remorse for his actions. Nero acted before the writing of John's Apocalypse; Pliny, after. Are we to believe that between these two horrific regional pogroms that Christians were held in high esteem? Absolutely not. This is not how social status and esteem work. It is how lasting prejudice and bigotry work.

Revelation is not alone in describing the Roman Empire as a hostile environment. The New Testament and early history of the church are replete with examples of prejudice and hostility toward this emerging form of Israel's faith. Matthew 5:11-12 reads, "Happy are you when people insult you and harass you and speak all kinds of bad and false things about you, all because of me. Be full of joy and be glad, because you have a great reward in heaven. In the same way, people harassed the prophets who came before you." John 15:19 reads similarly: "However, I have chosen you out of the world, and you don't belong to the world. This is why the world hates you." Acts contains many references to hostility against and persecution of Christians by both Jews and Gentiles. For example, "The apostles left the council rejoicing because they had been regarded as worthy to suffer disgrace for the sake of the name" (Acts 5:41). And writing from prison, Paul gives us these words:

> Do this so that you stand firm, united in one spirit and mind as you struggle together to remain faithful to the gospel. That way, you won't be afraid of anything your enemies do. Your faithfulness and courage are a sign of their coming destruction and your salvation, which is from God. God has generously granted you the privilege, not only of believing in Christ but also of suffering for Christ's sake. You are having the same struggle that you saw me face and now hear that I'm still facing. (Phil 1:27b-30)

There is a similar statement in 1 Peter 4:12-13, written to the same general region to which Revelation was sent, that says,

> Dear friends, don't be surprised about the fiery trials that have come among you to test you. These are not strange happenings. Instead, rejoice as you share Christ's suffering. You share his suffering now so that you may also have overwhelming joy when his glory is revealed.

One finds in *1 Clement* 5–6 mention of the persecution of Peter and Paul and also those who were their contemporaries. "Through jealousy and envy the greatest and most righteous pillars of the Church were persecuted and contended unto death."[44] Ignatius, whether he was a bishop or not, was martyred because he was a Christian.

These non-apocalyptic writings show that other Christians perceived Roman society as hostile to their community just as the prophet John did. Moreover, the passage from Phil 1:28 and 3:19 speak of the destruction of the enemies of Christians, an apocalyptic motif, in exhorting Christians to stand firmly in the faith. John was not the lone wolf some may argue that he was. He simply represented an apocalyptic version of what other first-century Christians experienced and expressed in other ways.

The letters are indeed introductions to the apocalyptic visions, but they are not merely prose versions of the apocalyptic visions. They are instructions aimed at enabling the churches to survive the apocalyptic trials that John envisions. They can do this by not giving in to social pressures to conform. Thus if Christians adhere to this advice, they will endure the trials and punishments described in the apocalyptic visions and enter the New Jerusalem. This argument explains both the function of Revelation 2–3 within the entire book, and also the theological connection between chapters 2–3 and Revelation 4–22.

Like the first-century realities that shaped John's Apocalypse, social pressure on minority groups is not foreign to America. Ways to alleviate those pressures also are not foreign. It is the Irish American Roman Catholic who moves from Albany, New York, to Albany, Georgia, and decides to become Episcopalian. It is Jewish American Hollywood producers in the middle of the twentieth century making idealistic movies about the American melting pot, in spite of being excluded from certain social circles.

44. "1 Clement," in *The Apostolic Fathers*, vol. 1, ed. Bart D. Ehrman, Loeb Classical Library 24 (Cambridge, MA: Harvard University Press, 2003), 5.2.

It is the bilingual Hispanic American who never speaks Spanish outside her home. It is the Italian American who anglicizes the pronunciation of his surname. These changes do not come in a vacuum. They constitute responses to social pressure and forms of survival-driven accommodation.

American Accommodations
Often during the twentieth century Americans with roots from central or eastern Europe either changed the pronunciation or the spelling of their surnames in order to fit in better in American society. Many southerners also sought to lose their accents in order to be better accepted in American society.

Christianity in the First Century

First-century Christians described the relations between Christians and pagans, on one front, and Jews, on another, in several writings. While these writings show that Christians in different contexts and times had different experiences, they also report that many of these experiences were negative.

First and foremost, several writers record that Christians suffered simply because of the name Christ/Christian. For example, Matthew 10:17-22 describe pagan and Jewish repression of Christians "on account of my name." In this context, Jesus predicts that his followers will be beaten, brought to trial "because of me," and that family members will betray one another. Some Christians will be executed simply "on account of the name."[45] One finds similar comments in Matthew 24:9, Luke 21:12, John 15:21, Acts 5:41, and 1 Peter 4:14. For example, Acts 5:17-42 is one of many passages in that book relating Christian suffering (e.g., 4:1-22; 6:8-8:1; 12:1-19; 16:16-40; 21:27-36; 23:12-22). Acts 5:41 aptly summarizes the passage: "The apostles left the council rejoicing because they had been regarded worthy to suffer disgrace for the sake of the name."[46] These narratives recur throughout the book of Acts in different localities.

45. Cf. Ian Boxall, *Discovering Matthew* (Grand Rapids: Eerdmans, 2015), 95.

46. Cf. C. S. Keener, *Acts: An Exegetical Commentary*, 4 vols. (Grand Rapids: Baker Academic, 2013), 2:1242–46. Keener entitles this section "Celebrating Persecution."

Moreover, pagan and Jewish harassment was felt so deeply by some Christians that they developed a rationale for Christian suffering empowering a greater missional confidence. For example, Paul wrote, "I want you to know, brothers, that my circumstances have turned out for the greater progress of the gospel, so that my imprisonment because of Christ has become well-known... and that most of the brothers, trusting in the Lord because of my imprisonment, dare to speak the word more abundantly without fear" (Phil 1:12-14 [author translation]; cf. Gal 1:13-14; 1 Pet 1:6-7; Rev 7:14).

Others went further and related Christ's suffering to their own experiences as a form of identification with, participation in, and continuation of their Savior's creation-changing work: "If the world hates you, know that it hated me first" (John 15:18; cf. Heb 12:3). First Peter 4:13 reads similarly: "Instead, rejoice as you share Christ's suffering. You share his suffering now so that you may also have overwhelming joy when his glory is revealed."[47] In some instances, Christians felt ostracized by the general society and frequently placed their local problems on a cosmic scale: "Don't be surprised, brothers and sisters, if the world hates you" (1 John 3:13) or "We found this man [i.e., Paul] to be a troublemaker who stirs up riots... throughout the empire" (Acts 24:5; see Acts 24:1-27 in its entirety). In the same general area as Revelation, 1 Pet 5:9 reads, "Resist him [i.e., the devil], standing firm in the faith. Do so in the knowledge that your fellow believers are enduring the same suffering throughout the world." In this regard, 1 Thessalonians 2:14-16 is particularly significant, because it refers to the repression of Christians at a time when some first-generation Christians were still alive. M. E. Boring reminds readers that "their suffering [i.e., the Thessalonians] corresponds to that of the earliest Christian believers in Judea, who suffered at the hands of their Judean neighbors."[48]

47. Cf. Rev 5:9-10. See also J. B. Green, *1 Peter*, THNTC (Grand Rapids: Eerdmans, 2007), 150–61.

48. M. E. Boring, *I & II Thessalonians: A Commentary*, NTL (Louisville: Westminster John Knox, 2015), 98; see also 97–108.

Rejoicing while Suffering

You now rejoice in this hope, even if it's necessary for you to be distressed for a short time by various trials. This is necessary so that your faith may be found genuine. (1 Pet 1:6-7a)

Still others sought and expected an imminent end to their trials, which would vindicate them, echoing apocalyptic themes (e.g., Matt 24:9-35; 1 Pet 1:6-12; 5:10). "When they harass you in one city, flee to the next. Let me assure you that you will not go through all the cities of Israel before the Son of Man comes" (Matt 10:23 [author translation]). "After you have suffered for a little while, the God of all grace, the one who called you into his eternal glory in Christ Jesus, will himself restore, empower, strengthen, and establish you" (1 Pet 5:10).

Several New Testament writings, dated variously by scholars from 55 to 125 CE, convey that Christians saw themselves as the True or New Israel that continues the task the Old Israel had left undone (e.g., Acts 13:46-48; 14:27; 24:10-16; 28:17-30; Gal 3:79; 6:16; Rom 4:13-17; Jas 1:1; cf. 1 Pet 1:1; 2:9-10; Rev 7:49). Revelation 2:9 and 3:9 reflect a social context where both sides called themselves Jews and thought of themselves as the elect people of God.[49] Thomas and Macchia write that "there is a tension between some of the churches of Revelation and the broader Jewish community, a tension that appears to revolve around the issue of identity of God's people."[50] This Christian self-image would not have endeared Christianity to other movements within Judaism. Other forms of Judaism would have reasserted their own claims to election, probably excluding Christians. Also, Gentile Christians claiming to be God's true people would have upset more traditional Jewish persons, many of whom thought of Gentiles as impure by nature.

The Book of Revelation deals with some of these same issues in very similar ways. Asian Christians addressed in Revelation suffered because they confessed the name Christ/Christian (e.g., Rev 2:17; 3:5, 10, 12). The book relates their sufferings to those of Christ (e.g., Rev 1:56; 5:9-10;

49. See my *Christ and Community*, 158–60.

50. Thomas and Macchia, *Revelation*, 96; see also 121–22. So too Blount, *Revelation*, 53–55.

7:14-17), thereby developing a christological rationale for Christian distress. Revelation also expected the oppression to end soon (e.g., Rev 1:3; 3:10; 22:10, 12, 20), placing those regional tensions that produced this suffering on a cosmic scale, because that is what an apocalypse does (Rev 4–19).

Indeed, one of the key issues for Revelation was how the Christian community should relate to the imperial cult.[51] Price argues that there was no Christian mechanism for showing respect to the emperor because Christianity had no role for sacrifice in its rituals. Conversely, adherents of the imperial cult expected some sign of reverence for the emperor that approximated sacrifice. At this point, Christian practice and pagan expectations generated tensions to the social detriment of the Christians. Pagans would have pressured the Christians to become more accommodating to ancient, regional religio-political customs.[52] I concur with Price. For these Christians, Christ had already performed the sacrifice (e.g., Mark 10:45; 1 Cor 11:25; Heb 9:11-14; Rev 1:5). Conversely, pressure on Christians to conform would have produced resistance in some and laxity and indulgence in others. At the same time, the Christian assertion that they were the true Israel and Christ Jesus was the divine Son of God would have caused tensions between Christian Jews and more traditional Jewish groups.

Roman writers did not hold Christians in high esteem. Even when they were sympathetic these same writers could describe Christians in very harsh terms.[53] In describing the repression of Christians following the burning of Rome in 64, Tacitus in *Annals* 15.44 has an enlightening passage on Roman attitudes toward Christians.

51. Price, *Rituals and Power*, 197–98; see also 123–26. See also Jerry L. Sumney, who argues that Roman society forced Christians to either acquiesce, accommodate, or stand firm in their beliefs and practices (*Colossians: A Commentary*. NTL [Louisville: Westminster John Knox, 2008], 15).

52. Price, *Rituals and Power*, 220–23.

53. E.g., M. E. Boring, *Revelation*, Interpretation (Louisville: Westminster John Knox, 1989), 8–23; Krodel, *Revelation*, 35–42; R. W. Wall, *Revelation*, NIBC (Peabody, MA: Hendrickson, 1991), 10–12. See also the work of the classicists Price, *Rituals and Power*, 197–98; and A. N. Sherwin White, *The Letters of Pliny: A Historical and Social Commentary* (Oxford: Clarendon, 1966), 772–87; cf. A. Y. Collins, *Crisis and Catharsis: The Power of the Apocalypse* (Philadelphia: Westminster, 1984), 84–110.

> Therefore, to scotch the rumor [that the fire had been started intentionally] Nero substituted as culprits, and punished with the utmost refinements of cruelty, a class of men, loathed for their vices, whom the crowd styled the Christians. Christus, the founder of the name [*nomen*], had undergone the death penalty in the reign of Tiberius, by sentence of the procurator Pontius Pilate, and the pernicious superstition was checked for a moment, only to break out once more, not merely in Judaea, the home of the disease, but in the capital itself. . . . First, then, the confessed members of the sect were arrested; next, on their disclosures, vast numbers were convicted, not so much on the count of arson as for hatred of the human race.[54]

While Tacitus clearly decries Nero's action, he has no love for Christians. He refers to their faith as a superstition and a disease. Moreover, Christians were deemed guilty simply because they were Christians. These highly anti-Christian sentiments reflect a general lack of respect for Christians altogether in Roman society (cf. Matt 10:17-23; John 15:21; Acts 5:41; 1 Pet 4:14; Rev 2:17; 3:5, 10, 12). Suetonius makes a similar comment in his *Nero* 16.2: "Punishment was inflicted on the Christians, a class of men given to a new and mischievous superstition." This is not high esteem. It is bigotry, an unwarranted and unjustified disregard for a specific group of human beings. And it is stubborn in its dismissal. Heller states the case succinctly: "In vain do we confront the established prejudices with reality: they are unshakeable."[55]

Several New Testament and classical commentators have argued that a sporadic regional suppression of Christians in Roman Asia in the first century CE is historically significant and intelligible.[56] Furthermore, these exegetes state that such limited actions could be as horrific as an imperial persecution to those who suffered its effects. They postulate that John placed a regional repression of Christians on a cosmic scale in order to explain the plight of his fellow Christians within the wider perspective of the divine plan. Indeed, persons undergoing cultural or ethnic discrimination

54. Tacitus, *Annals*, Books 13–16, trans. John Jackson, Loeb Classical Library 322 (Cambridge, MA: Harvard University Press, 1937).

55. A. Heller, "Toward a Sociology of Knowledge of Everyday Life," *Cultural Hermeneutics* 3 (1975): 10.

56. E.g., Yarbro Collins, *Crisis*, 84–110; Boring, *Revelation*, 8–23; Price, *Rituals and Power*, 123–26. See also Friesen's *Imperial Cults and the Apocalypse of John*.

around the world know too well that regional suffering is no less horrific than global suffering. In other words, bigotry might remain suspended until its proponents felt threatened or felt bold enough to act without fear.

Regional Repression

Examples of regional repression in the last one hundred years would include Catholics in Northern Ireland, the Basques in Spain, Bantu in South Africa, and Native Americans in North and South America.

This reading of Revelation provides a needed corrective to the assumption that since there was no empire-wide persecution that there was no suffering. Further, this position relates John's Apocalypse to first- and early second-century CE Christian and Roman writers who describe the low social status of Christians. Indeed, Christians suffered not because of their criminality but often merely because of what people thought of them. Additionally, our sources show that both Jews and pagans had reasons to resent Christians and to see them as social deviants.

While the previous section looked at the social status of Christians in the late first and early second century in Asia, this section reveals that both the novelty of Christianity and its Asian religio-political context itself would have caused significant tensions between Christians and pagans. Christians were perceived negatively because of their refusal to participate in the imperial cult.[57]

The Power of Symbols

Symbols and symbolic acts are extremely important in human societies. Symbols constitute shorthand representations of group identities or group values. Thus, to disrespect the symbol shows disrespect for that which the symbol represents. Respecting the symbol shows esteem for that which the symbol represents. That is why people become angry when they perceive someone disrespecting national symbols. However, peaceful protests are appropriate when the values that the symbols represent are not applied equally and indiscriminately.

57. Price, *Rituals and Power*, 123–26.

Greco-Roman society in general had little respect for new movements. The Roman state in particular was suspicious of any new assembly or association, lest it might develop into a political organization in conflict with the Roman state.[58] Second, and perhaps more important, the Asian religio-political setting itself could produce tensions between non-Christians who participated in the imperial cult and Christians who did not. In the eastern region of the Mediterranean, the worship of the emperor was not mandated by the emperor himself but was a spontaneous grassroots movement among the common people, who traditionally believed that the king was a son of the nation's god.[59] Alexander received such treatment after conquering these countries as well as his Seleucid and Ptolemaic successors.

When the Romans conquered the eastern Mediterranean, their emperors received similar divine honors.[60] The Roman imperial cult began in Asia in the first century BCE. Dio Cassius writes that early in Augustus's principate, Roman citizens in Asia were required to worship the divine Julius Caesar and the goddess Roma, while the provincials were required to worship Augustus and the goddess Roma, the patron goddess of Rome.[61] Pausanias mentions a temple to Octavia, Augustus's sister, in the first century BCE. Claudius's living grandmother was worshiped as *Thea Antonia*.[62] Although Caligula might have been the first living emperor to require worship, he was not the first living member of the imperial family to receive divine honors. Price's comment is important: "Though I would not wish to return to the old picture of a clash between Christ and the Caesars, the imperial cult was clearly one of the features of the contemporary world that troubled the Christians. Their responses during the first three centuries of the empire consisted essentially of passive resistance."[63]

58. E.g., Pliny, *Letter*, 10.96–97. See also R. Stark, "The Class Basis of Early Christianity from a Sociological Model," *Sociological Analysis* 47 (1986): 225.

59. See Price, *Rituals and Power*, 123–26; 197–98; 220–22.

60. See Plutarch, *Lysander*, 18, and *Dion*, 29; F. W. Walbank, *The Hellenistic World* (Cambridge, MA: Harvard University Press, 1982), 209–26; Price, *Rituals and Power*, 25–47. This is not to say that there was an unbroken, identical tradition between the Hellenistic ruler cults and the Roman imperial cult. Rather, I am here referring to continuities between the two (cf. Price, *Rituals and Power*, 23–25).

61. *Roman Histories* 51.20.67.

62. N. Kokkinos, *Antonia Augusta: Portrait of a Great Lady* (London: Routledge, 1992), 158–62.

63. Price, *Rituals and Power*, 123; cf. Blount, *Revelation*, 58; Thomas and Macchia, *Revelation*, 118–26.

The imperial cult was practiced reverently in Asia and in most of the eastern Mediterranean region of the Roman Empire. Moreover, cities competed vigorously for the privilege of being declared *neokoros*, an official site for the imperial cult. All seven cities addressed in Revelation 2–3 received this honor in the first or early second century CE.[64] In the first century CE, Ephesus (see Rev 2:1), which was designated as an official site of the imperial cult more than once, had a cult to Roma and Julius Caesar and later added a temple to Tiberius. Caesarea had a temple to Augustus and Roma. Pilate dedicated a shrine in Caesarea to Tiberius. Augustus was worshiped in Antioch near Pisidia in his lifetime. Other first-century CE neokorate cities included Pergamum, Smyrna, Sardis, Laodicea, Philadelphia (all mentioned in Rev 2–3), Cyzicus, and Ancyra.[65]

Becoming an official center of the imperial cult symbolized for these cities civic pride and devotion to their religio-political traditions. It also created social bonds that led to social benefits, such as building projects and help after natural disasters. Perhaps more important, the imperial cult established a means by which these cities came to understand their relationship to the new Roman imperial power by representing it in long-established traditions.[66] The imperial cult played a key role in the establishment of the new symbolic universe for the Roman province of Asia. Christians who denied the validity of these religio-political traditions constituted an affront to Asian pagan social sensibilities. Christian religious impiety, from a pagan perspective, left these cities open to reprisals from the gods through natural disasters and social anarchy.[67]

S. J. Friesen's work is very helpful in helping us to understand the social setting, how and why the imperial cult developed, the social and psychological needs it met, and how it impacted life in the region. He illuminates how the imperial cult fit into Asian cosmogony, cosmology,

64. See, e.g., Price, *Rituals and Power*, 24–25, 249–74; J. Ferguson, *The Religions of the Roman Empire* (Surrey: Thames & Hudson, 1970), 93–98.

65. See Price, *Rituals and Power*, xxii–xxvi; 64–67; 249–74.

66. Price, *Rituals and Power*, 25, 51–58, 171, 225–27, 239–48.

67. This is similar to how some contemporary Christians connect natural and human-made disasters as a consequence of moral problems in American society.

and imperial history—the sacred stories that gave meaning to life. Cosmogony, a creation story, played no direct role in the development of ruler cults in Roman Asia. However, individuals in the imperial family were identified with deities in the Olympian pantheon, "thereby tying them indirectly into the mythic narratives of the origins of the world."[68] This practice explained the role of the imperial family with the Olympians and made sense to Asians. It established a connection between antiquity and the present and conveyed that the imperial family was predetermined by the gods. Second, Caesar Augustus, working within the context of Olympian religion, brought forth a new world order supposedly ordained by the gods. Augustus in his very person made the will of the gods manifest in human history: he brought peace and order. Thus, Augustus and also his dynastic line were predestined to rule.[69] And Caesar Augustus's birthday became an empire-wide holiday. For centuries, rulers in this general region who created social order were often viewed as social benefactors for their given communities and they often were described as "divine men," persons with extraordinary gifts.[70]

Cosmology, a story about the structure of the world, "defined how space and time were to be experienced."[71] Rome became the mythic center of the universe. Cities could establish their own sites of the imperial cult, but they would not have the full backing of the emperor or the Roman Senate. Locally established cults reflected more local customs and traditions and not Roman ones. However, provincial sites of imperial cults had to be approved by the imperial office and the Roman Senate had to incorporate Roman ideas, honors, and practices. Furthermore, the presence of a provincial site enhanced a city's status within the province itself. It denoted the importance of the city and cities vied for the honor. This honor also brought other social benefactions, like building projects and help after disasters. Friesen adds that while it is true that many persons

68. Friesen, *Imperial Cults and the Apocalypse*, 123.

69. The pervasive influence of astrology and Stoicism, which both affirmed a predestined world order, reinforced the myth of Roman hegemony.

70. Cf. Charles Talbert, *What Is a Gospel?* (Philadelphia: Fortress, 1977).

71. Friesen, *Imperial Cults and the Apocalypse*, 124.

besides the emperor received divine honors, all the honorees were Romans. Rome remained the center of the focus.

Along with sacred geography came sacred history. Asian calendars were aligned with the Roman calendar. The empire gave time meaning. Specifically, the birth and accomplishments of Caesar Augustus gave time meaning. "Augustus was a cosmogonic and cosmological deity," Friesen writes. He continues, "Augustus would make sense of time."[72] Festivals throughout the calendar established cycles of rest, commemoration, entertainment, and competition that gave a sense of uniformity to life. Local traditions stood alongside imperial traditions, coalescing both into one new social matrix. Every level of Asian society was impacted as persons from every social strata found a way to participate in the religio-political context. "In any case, the calendar drew members into a series of celebrations that covered a range of human experiences."[73] The imperial cult was not limited to a single dynastic family because the cult was so closely tied to the continuation of the empire. "The emperors, their families, the Senate, and the city of Rome had redefined the structure of life in the Mediterranean world."[74]

Sacred Hierarchies

Sacred stories—narratives that relate the activities of divine beings—both form and inform human institutions. Because they are deemed sacred, humans often model their own social groups after the heavenly, sacred patterns depicted in these narratives. For example, ancient Israel and the early Christian churches emerged among mythologies in the ancient Near East, which envisioned their deity enthroned in heaven surrounded by a multitude of semidivine beings. By the period between the Old and New Testaments, the more important beings or divine messengers, for some cultures called "archangels," sat closest to God. The closer one sat to God, the more important one was. God sat on the throne in the middle and all look up to God. We repeat this authority pattern in the cabinets of most major governments, for example, the United States, Great Britain, and Germany, to name but a few. Boards of directors of major corporations have the same pattern. And fathers often take their place at the head of the table. We cause a fuss if a leader were to sit anywhere else, as if one loses power by choosing another seat. And we think nothing of it. It is "natural," so we think.

72. Friesen, *Imperial Cults and the Apocalypse*, 125.

73. Friesen, *Imperial Cults and the Apocalypse*, 126.

74. Friesen, *Imperial Cults and the Apocalypse*, 127.

Eschatology, which is often expressed through a story explaining the end of time, had both personal and cosmic aspects. Personal aspects included descriptions of the afterlife, funerals, and discussions of the best way(s) to face death. These features merged most clearly in the deification of a deceased Roman emperor, where "personal eschatology intersected with imperial cults."[75] While Jewish and Christian eschatology looked forward to the end of this world, Roman cosmic eschatology "allowed for no termination of the world."[76] The cult continued the veneration of the empire through veneration of each generation of the imperial family, ensuring proper respect for whomever the future emperor might be. "In this case, the Roman Empire constituted a utopian vision that had the misfortune of succeeding."[77] Many persons within the empire overlooked the inconsistency of bestowing immortality to inevitably flawed human institutions because reasons to participate were too ingrained into Asian society. "This tension between cosmology and eschatology . . . provided the matrix within which John's religious criticism could take root."[78]

Therefore, the imperial cult gave meaning and structure to life in the Roman province of Asia, a region where the worship of the ruler was deeply ingrained in the social fabric. It explained why the Roman Empire was preordained by the Olympian gods, how Caesar Augustus brought the will of the gods into being, and how the empire that gave the world peace and order was a utopian state and the goal of human history. Into this cultural mix, John brings an alternate vision of the Roman Empire: it is a beast that oppresses, exploits, and kills the saints. For John, the utopian state is yet to come and will not come from humans who assume divine honors, but it will come from the true ruler of the cosmos who comes in disguise as a slain lamb.

In this introduction to the cultural context of the Book of Revelation, first, we stressed that an apocalypse is a literary genre that has several key features, but that not every apocalypse shares all these features. There is

75. Friesen, *Imperial Cults and the Apocalypse*, 130.

76. Friesen, *Imperial Cults and the Apocalypse*, 130.

77. Friesen, *Imperial Cults and the Apocalypse*, 131.

78. Friesen, *Imperial Cults and the Apocalypse*, 131.

variety within the genre, giving each apocalypse a uniqueness. Second, we argued that the internal evidence of John's Apocalypse indicates a likely 68–70 CE date of composition. Additionally, John's Apocalypse is an example of Christian Judaism, coming from a time when Christianity was still a movement within Judaism. Third, the writings of both Romans and Christians show that Christians were held in low esteem in the first Christian century. Moreover, evidence of this in Revelation 2–3 has been overlooked by many New Testament scholars. In conjunction with misreadings of Revelation 2–3, many have not adequately factored in how bias against an entire group works in human societies. The previous section looked at several early Christian writings (which were not apocalypses) that described Roman society as a hostile environment for Christians. In Roman Asia, these pressures came from other Jewish groups as well as non-Jewish residents of Asia. Finally, this chapter examined how the imperial cult made sense of the world and history for the Roman province of Asia and touched every level of society.

In the next chapter, we will discuss the Lamb as the most pervasive image of Christ in the Book of Revelation. It will show how the old image of the Lion of David has been replaced by the Lamb and how witnessing, not warfare, became the means of victory over evil in a repressive empire.

Study Questions

1. How is John's Apocalypse unique, and why does it matter?
2. Do you think the date of John's Apocalypse matters?
3. Give examples of why social bias has a long shelf life.
4. What surprised you about why the imperial cult had meaning for Asians? Are there any parallels with Christianity?
5. What is the difference between separation of church and state *and* separation of religion and state? Which is true in this country?

Chapter 2

WORTHY IS THE LAMB

In this chapter we examine the role and function of the slain Lamb as the most pervasive and developed christological image found in the Book of Revelation. The slain Lamb replaces the Lion of David, a traditional Jewish messianic image found in 2 Esdras 11–12 and *Testament of Judah* 24. This change reflects the church's response to the historical fact that the Christian Messiah has died an unjust, humiliating death. The crucifixion and the resurrection have powerfully reshaped the Christology of the Book of Revelation by redefining victory as victory through suffering, the opposite of what was expected by more traditional Jews and also the opposite of Greco-Roman expectations of a true leader. It may also reflect the continuing struggle of the community in a polytheistic culture and the martyrdoms of Christian leaders such as Peter and Paul, on the one hand, and the delay of the return of Christ who will save the faithful, on the other.

The Images of Christ

The three major images of Christ in Revelation are the Human One/ Son of Man (see the CEB translation), the slain Lamb, and the Divine Warrior. The roots of the Messiah as an apocalyptic human being have a lengthy history, one that is more tedious in the academy than the religious tradition itself. Too much confusion exists between the generic phrase *son of man*, which in Hebrew or Aramaic idiom means "human being," and comparisons rendered as "one like a son of man" (Dan 7:13;

Rev 1:13; cf. 1 En. 46:1). The generic idiom refers to human beings; the comparisons refer to titles for heavenly beings in human form. These heavenly beings are the deity in human form (e.g., Ezek 1:26), an archangel in human form (e.g., Dan 10:16, 18) or the messiah in human form (2 Esd 13:3).[1]

While the Divine Warrior (DW) in Revelation 19 has its roots in ancient Near Eastern mythology, Revelation 19 reflects the more immediate influence of Isaiah 63. Judaism embraced the DW image and applied it to various contexts. One finds four major motifs in this portrait. First, God Almighty is "Lord of heavenly forces" *(YHWH Sabaoth)*. This is an image of God as one who makes war against the enemies of Israel accompanied by a heavenly army (e.g., 1 Sam 15:2; Zech 11:1-6). Second, God also slays the sea monster and brings order from chaos (e.g., Ps 74:13-14; Isa 27:1). This is an Israelite version of an ancient creation story (the Mesopotamian Enuma Elish). Third, God judges and punishes evil wherever it may be found (e.g., Hag 1:5-11; Isa 3:1-15). And finally, the Divine Warrior liberates his people (Exod 14:1-15; Isa 35; 40:3).

Revelation 19:11-21 contains the heavenly forces and the punishing judger, but probably not the sea monster, though the beast is a monster. John reinterprets them in such a way that the motifs never become stagnant idols but sustain a fresh application. They are ancient but become a new means of communication. The principle Divine Warrior model for Revelation 19:11-21 is Isaiah 63:1-6. In Isaiah 63:1-6, God comes to purify Zion and to punish those nations who have taken advantage of their political dominance of Israel. God acts alone because only God has the power to bring justice and vindication to his people. Often Jewish and Christian apocalyptic writers believed only God could vindicate God's people. Indeed, many Christians see contemporary times as so spiritually decadent that Christ's return must be soon.

1. For my complete argument, see my "Son of Man" article in *Oxford Encyclopedia of the Bible and Theology*, ed. Samuel E. Balentine, 2 vols. (Oxford: Oxford University Press, 2015), 2:316–21, and my *The Son of Man in Second Temple Judaism: Reviewing and Advancing the Scholarly Debate*, Frontiers of Scholarly Research (Lewiston, NY: Mellen, 2017).

God as Divine Warrior

Who is this coming from Edom,
  from Bozrah in bright red garments,
  this splendidly dressed one, striding with great power?
  It is I, proclaiming righteousness, powerful to save! (Isa 63:1)

Christology in John's Apocalypse

The Christology of John's Apocalypse communicated five basic truths to the original recipients. First and foremost, it communicated to Asian Christians under Roman rule that Christ was the Lord of the cosmos with whom God Almighty shared divine honors (e.g., Rev 1:8, 17-18; 19:11; 21:5; 22:6). Throughout the visions, John stresses Christ's faithful witness to God Almighty and thus validates his worthiness to participate in divine honors. Christ is the personification of "the Word of God" (19:13). Several confirmation statements do this by creating a parallel between God's word and Jesus's witness to God. For example, in Revelation 1:2, 9 and 20:4 we find the exact same words in Greek: "the word of God and the witness of Jesus" (author translation). The message here is that there is no difference between God's word and Jesus's witness. Asian Christians should remain secure that if their witness remains consistent with the witness of Jesus that they shall overcome as Jesus has overcome.

That is exactly what one finds in Revelation 6:9-10, where we see a parallel between God's word and the community's witness:

> When he opened the fifth seal, I saw under the altar those who had been slaughtered on account of the word of God and the witness they had given. They cried out with a loud voice, "Holy and true Master, how long will you wait before you pass judgment? How long before you require justice for our blood, which was shed by those who live on earth?"

For the Asian Christian community, this would have conveyed that consistency with the word of God would bring suffering, but endurance through this suffering would ultimately bring vindication as well. Or as M. Eugene Boring reminds readers, "The chopping block of the Roman executioner has become a cosmic altar. Christians who refuse to sacrifice to the image of the Emperor are nonetheless Christian priests who sacrifice themselves on the true altar of God."[2] Victory through suffering—first in Christ, then in the martyrs—is the means of overcoming evil in the world. Moreover, the martyrs must ask when God will vindicate them, a job that only God can perform.

Second, Christ, functioning as God's divine agent and judge, defeats the enemies of God and God's people (e.g., Rev 19:11-21). It is significant that Jesus did not choose expediency but faithfulness and thus redefined victory. The faithful followers of Christ will conquer in the same way. The followers of the Lamb belong to God Almighty. So the appropriate response "is seen in their remaining 'faithful' to God in the midst of temptation and persecution, with Jesus as 'faithful witness' as their model and their own 'faithfulness' as the result. In other words, participation in the heavenly army demands lives of faithfulness to the 'commands of God and the testimony of Jesus.'"[3]

Third, Christ leads an eschatological community of priest-kings to the New Jerusalem (e.g., 1:6; 7:1-17; 14:1-5; 19:1-10). They represent the perfect community of the elect and gather on Mount Zion (7:5-8; 14:1-5). This is an appropriation of the exodus motif. Those who have been faithful until the end shall reign with Christ in the New Jerusalem (see 20:4-6). This symbolized the vindication of the faithful at Christ's return. The Lamb has oversight over the book of life and who will enter the New Jerusalem (13:8; 17:8, 14). None who have not been faithful will gain entry.[4] This exodus motif would have given assurance to its intended audience that faithfulness will not go unrewarded. These first three motifs—Christ as cosmic Lord, vanquisher of God's/the people's enemies, leader

2. M. E. Boring, *Revelation*, Interpretation (Louisville: Westminster John Knox, 1989), 125.

3. Grant R. Osborne, *Revelation*, BECNT (Grand Rapids: Baker Academic, 2002), 624. The "commands of God" in 12:17 and 14:12 are synonymous with the expression "the word of God" found in 1:9, 6:9, and 20:4. Perhaps "through the word of their witness" in 12:11 may also belong on this list (translation is mine in this footnote).

4. Cf. Richard Bauckham, *The Theology of the Book of Revelation* (New York: Cambridge University Press, 1993), 70–72. See also F. J. Murphy, *Fallen Is Babylon: The Revelation to John* (Harrisburg, PA: Trinity, 1998), 192–200.

of priests/kings into the New Jerusalem—are interlocked and should be viewed as mutually inclusive.

Heavenly Records

But I will tell you what is written in the Scroll of Truth. (Dan 10:21)

Then the king will say to those on his right, "Come, you who will receive good things from my Father. Inherit the kingdom that was prepared for you before the world began." (Matt 25:34)

And the judge said to one of the angels that was waiting on him, "Open this book for me and find me the sins of this soul." (*T.Abr.* 12:17)[5]

A victory-through-suffering theme is associated with all three images of Christ (1:5-6; 5:9-10; 19:13).[6] This motif reflects a community suffering under regional repression for its religious beliefs. John's visions turn their affliction into their means of salvation and coping. Revelation was not the only New Testament book to make this transformation. For example, Philippians 1:13 reads, "The whole Praetorian Guard and everyone else knows that I'm in prison for Christ." One finds similar sentiments in James 1:2-3 and 1 Peter 1:6-7—and throughout the book of Acts Christians suffer for their beliefs (e.g., 6:8–8:1; 12:1-9; 21:27–22:29). Such statements reflect a lack of respect for Christians in the broader Roman society, given that these writings come from separate contexts.[7]

Finally, the Human One/Son of Man and the Lamb images are more pastoral than the Divine Warrior, who functions primarily as an eschatological judge, while still incorporating features from the first two images. This points to the multifaceted nature of the Christology of Revelation. While the first two images concern themselves with protecting, nurturing, and comforting the community, the Divine Warrior acts as an eschatological judge who vindicates the community of the faithful. Sophie

5. N. Turner, trans., "The Testament of Abraham," *AOT.*

6. I am one who believes that the blood on the Divine Warrior's robe in 19:13 is Christ's blood because Christ overcomes by shedding his blood in John's Apocalypse (e.g., 1:5; 5:9-10; 12:11).

7. See my more complete discussion of first-century responses to Christianity in Thomas B. Slater, *Christ and Community: A Socio-Historical Study of the Christology of Revelation*, JSNTSup (Sheffield, UK: Sheffield Academic, 1999), 18–22.

Laws observes how all three images reinforce one another. She notes that all three are messianic concepts and that Christ is understood "in terms of the character of God."[8] Communal cohesiveness is the key underlying motivation behind all three christological images.[9]

ANOTHER INTERPRETATION OF DANIEL 7:13
After seven days, I had a dream during the night. I looked and saw a wind rising from the sea. . . . As I watched, this wind made something like the figure of a man come up out of the heart of the sea. (2 Esd 13:1-3)

Christ the Slain Lamb

Without a doubt, the most extensive and intensive messianic image is the slain Lamb. While one finds the Human One/Son of Man concept in Revelation 1–3 and 14, and the Divine Warrior in Revelation 19:11-21, the image of the slain Lamb appears in Revelation 5 and recurs throughout the book.

The lamb imagery in Revelation also has roots in the Jewish sacrificial system and also Jewish apocalypticism. The Hebrew Bible has over four hundred references to rams, sheep, and lambs. The passages fall into two broad categories: the generic and the sacrificial. In generic references, the animal has no ceremonial or theological function. These are merely references to pastoral animals. For example, "Jacob said, 'Don't pay me anything. If you will do this for me, I will take care of your flock again" (Gen 30:31). The sacrificial passages, however, contain theological elements. In Exodus 12:2-12, one finds instructions for selecting an animal worthy for sacrifice for the first Passover. Isaiah 1:11 gives us a striking example of YHWH's disdain for the abuse of the sacrificial system (due to the neglect of justice):

> I'm fed up with entirely burned offerings of rams
> and the fat of well-fed beasts.
> I don't want the blood of bulls, lambs, and goats.

8. Sophie Laws, *In Light of the Lamb*, GNS 31 (Wilmington, DE: Michael Glazier, 1988), 26.

9. See Slater, *Christ and Community*, 236–45.

Second Temple Jewish apocalypticism added dimensions of power to the imagery. First Enoch 90:9 reads, "And I looked until the time that {thirty-seven} shepherds had pastured (the sheep) in the same way."[10] Here, as well as in verses 29-34, the sheep represent the Maccabees as righteous warriors against an evil Syrian empire. In the *Testament of Joseph* 19:8-9, a lamb as a messianic figure destroys the enemies of Israel. While these writings would have been current in Jewish apocalyptic circles and contributed to readers easily interpreting the Lamb as a messianic image, the *slain* Lamb would have still been unique in Revelation and the Gospels, because the Lamb conquers through suffering.

The crucifixion and the exaltation of Jesus provided a final, Christian element: the motif of victory through suffering. Victory through suffering then becomes the model for Asian Christians' behavior during their own regional repression. This motif is used by the writer of John's Apocalypse with sober reflection. Revelation reveals the conviction that the Messiah died an unjust, humiliating death and still overcame, and that Christians could become victors by following Christ's example.

The slain Lamb occurs twenty-eight times in twenty-seven passages from Revelation 5 to 22 in eleven separate contexts, and has similarities with other New Testament witnesses (e.g., John 1:29; Acts 8:32-35; 1 Cor 5:7; 1 Pet 1:19). Moreover, the slain Lamb performs several functions for the eschatological community. The variety of tasks demonstrates the width and breadth of the concept. Only the Lamb has conquered and been found worthy to open the scroll in Revelation 4:1–5:14. It is significant that the slain Lamb replaced the Lion, a traditional image found in Genesis 49:8-12, Testament of Judah 24, and 2 Esdras 11–12, because not only Jewish persons but all of Roman society looked for leaders who conquered through power: they looked for lions for leadership roles, not the vanquished, not slain lambs.[11] Just as G. K. Beale reminds readers, "The theme of this chapter is that Christ, as a Lion, overcame by being

10. M. A. Knibb, trans., "1 Enoch," *AOT*.

11. S. J. Friesen, *Imperial Cults and the Apocalypse of John* (Oxford: Oxford University Press, 2001), 199–201.

slaughtered as a Lamb. This is confirmed... (and) is a basis for His worthiness and thus also for His overcoming."[12]

A Hymn on Sacrifice

Here I raise mine Ebenezer; hither by thy help I'm come;
And I hope, by thy good pleasure, safely to arrive at home.
Jesus sought me when a stranger, wandering from the fold of God;
He, to rescue me from danger, interposed his precious blood.

—*Hymn, "Come, Thou Fount of Every Blessing," verse 2*

The Christ-Lamb performs five major functions for the Christian community. They all center on leading an eschatological exodus to the New Jerusalem (e.g., Rev 7:9-17; 14:1-5; 21:9–22:5). Within this scheme, the church constitutes a New Israel, a new international, multicultural community of faith (7:1-10). The Lamb is the ruler of the cosmos through suffering (17:14; 19:16) and those who follow his example will be redeemed by him at the eschatological judgment. This messianic image would have enabled the original audience to identify with Christ in a way that would have strengthened them during their own trials. *There is no rapture in John's Apocalypse.* Everyone must endure the suffering.

The first function of the Lamb was leading the eschatological community to the New Jerusalem and protecting it along the way. First and foremost, the death of the Lamb brings salvation to the faithful. The Lamb redeems an international, multiethnic community of the faithful through his sacrificial death, making them priest-kings, coregents with the divine who have access to the Godhead (Rev 1:5; 5:9; 7:14). As G. K. Beale so eloquently states,

> The redemption or purchase of men [and women] from every tribe and tongue and people and nation is a redemption designed to save some from throughout the people groups of the world. It is a redemption without dis-

12. G. K. Beale, *Revelation: A Shorter Commentary*, with David H. Campbell (Grand Rapids: Eerdmans, 2015), 114–15; cf. Craig R. Koester, *Revelation: A New Translation with Introduction and Commentary*, AB (New Haven, CT: Yale University Press, 2014), 386–87.

tinction, not a redemption without exception (people from all races), as 14:3-4, 6 will make clear.[13]

Revelation 12:1-11 states that the defeat of Satan in heaven by Michael and his angels came about because of the sacrificial death of the Lamb, which is already an accomplished fact. "The victory won over Satan reflected in this verse is not only a victory in heaven but also one that is already won on earth through martyrdom; it is not a victory that will be won in the future but one that is already a part of past experience."[14] Satan's subsequent fall from heaven is a precursor of Satan's fall on earth (19:11-21) and ultimate final fall (20:7-10). And the Lamb's sacrificial death is matched by the witness of the saints (12:10-12).[15]

This function also involves the Lamb protecting the community and defeating its enemies. The community will no longer suffer from the natural elements but will find eternal sustenance under the Lamb's pastoral care (7:16-17).[16] He seals the elect and protects them from the eschatological woes (7:1-8; 14:1-5). Moreover, the Lamb and the saints observe the eternal punishment of those who have persecuted the people of God (14:10). These passages would assure Asian Christians of their ultimate vindication and salvation. In the end, the Lamb will bestow positions of honor upon those who have suffered the most for their faithfulness (e.g., 12:11; 14:1-5; 17:14; 20:4-6).

The second function shows the Lamb's concern for the community. Only the Lamb is worthy to open the scroll that contains God Almighty's eschatological plans. By opening the scroll, the Lamb initiates the series of events that will lead to the ultimate salvation and victory of the people of God (5:9-10; 7:9-10; 19:5-10). Although the literary cycle of seals functions as a revelatory action, it will bring about a soteriological result for the

13. Beale, *Revelation*, 117.

14. D. E. Aune, *Revelation*. WBC 52 A–C (3 vols.) (Nashville: Thomas Nelson, 1997, 1998), 2:703.

15. Aune notes parallels to choosing death over accommodation to social pressures in Philo, *Leg.* 369, Mark 8:35, Matt 10:39, Luke 10:27, Eph 5:28, 1 Pet 3:10, Jos., *A.J.* 17.180, Ign. *Eph.* 9:3 (Aune, *Revelation* 2:703). This is a wide range of first-century Jewish and Christian writings. It illustrates how widespread disdain for Jews was at the time.

16. Cf. Stephen Pattemore, *The People of God in the Apocalypse: Discourse, Structure and Exegesis*, SNTSMS 128 (Cambridge: Cambridge University Press, 2004), 140–59.

faithful. Indeed, the Lamb is worthy because he has died a sacrificial death that, for suffering Christians, becomes a means of identification with their Lord and also a symbol of victory over sin and evil. One purpose of the Lamb imagery would then be to encourage Christians to remain true to their faith and thus overcome as the Christ-Lamb has overcome.[17] Brian Blount writes,

> John was essentially ordering his Christians to be about the business of telling on themselves, with full knowledge of the repercussions such telling might bring (recall Pliny's letter). He was asking them to come screaming out of the Christian closet, knowing that it could well solicit the same consequence it had attracted to the Lamb: slaughter.[18]

However, this type of witnessing was, from John's perspective, necessary and unavoidable if one were to be saved.

Determinism (or some prefer "assurance") is the third significant function of the Lamb. Determinism in apocalyptic writings has two interwoven purposes: assurance and exultation. It assures its readers of victory and encourages them to keep the faith.

The Lamb's scroll of life contains the names of citizens of the New Jerusalem, the most important deterministic feature in John's Apocalypse. The enrollment in the scroll of life assures the community of its salvation and the condemnation of its opponents. Names have been included in the scroll of life "from the time the earth was made" (13:8; 17:8). At once, it communicates assurance and judgment.

Fourth, the Lamb makes war against the enemies of God on earth and defeats them (12:10-12; 17:14). These passages are prolepses of the victory of the Divine Warrior in 19:11-21, the first of two defeats of Satan on earth. The use of military imagery suggests two conflicting, uncompromising groups that see nothing in common. Furthermore, military imagery is part and parcel of Second Temple Jewish apocalypticism (e.g., 1 En. 1:9; 10; 2 Esd 11–13). It conveyed the intensity of the conflict and also the finality of victory (cf. 1 En. 54–56; Apoc. Pet. 4–6). The military

17. Cf. Pattemore, *People of God*, 164–96.

18. B. K. Blount, *Revelation: A Commentary*, NTL (Louisville: Westminster John Knox, 2009), 13.

imagery does not connote Christian laxity but Christian fidelity. It meant that Christians were up against a powerful opponent, and victory would take the same type of mental toughness that war requires. Revelation encourages militant vigilance without engaging in war.

JUDGMENT
And behold! He comes with ten thousand holy ones to execute judgement upon them, and to destroy the impious, and to contend with all flesh concerning everything which the sinners and the impious have done and wrought against him. (1 En. 1:9)[19]

The fifth and final function conveys an important and unique concept: the unity of God Almighty, the Lamb, and the Christian martyrs. In the New Jerusalem, God Almighty and the Lamb constitute the center of life and religious activity, illuminate the city, provide the sustenance of life and eradicate all forms of disease (21:1–22:5). However, the visions never separate God Almighty and the Lamb, on the divine side, from the earthly community, on the human side. For example, the martyrs will sit on thrones with the Lamb (20:4-6). Confirmation statements ("the word of God and my witness about Jesus" [1:9] or "the word of God and the witness they had" [6:9]) functioned in this very same way. These statements serve to connect the earthly community with the heavenly community by connoting that the witness of Christians faithfully followed God's word and Christ's witness (see also 1:2; 12:11, 17; 14:12; 20:4).[20] The saints have the Lamb's/God's name on their foreheads (7:3 and 14:1), symbolizing both divine adoption and divine protection. The wedding banquet unites the Lamb and his bride, the saints (19:5-10), connoting an intimate relationship between the two. God Almighty personally wipes away the tears of the saints and prepares a home for them (7:17; 21:4). This would have spoken volumes in Greco-Roman society where the traditional gods were considered aloof, uncaring, and removed, while at the

19. Knibb, "1 Enoch."

20. It is probably not coincidental that there are seven such confirmation statements. Seven is a holy number in Revelation: seven letters to seven churches, seven seals, seven trumpets, seven bowls, seven beatitudes are a few examples.

same time resonating with the mystery religions where the god/goddess was viewed as immanent, caring, and involved in human life. All these things connoted to Asian Christians that if they were faithful to Christ Jesus, who was faithful to God Almighty, that ultimately they would have an unbroken, eternal fellowship with God Almighty and the Lamb in the New Jerusalem.[21]

Some of the significant passages embodying these testimonial functions bear a closer look. We turn first to Revelation 4–5, the initial presentation of the slain Lamb. This vision sets the stage for the Christology, soteriology, and ecclesiology for the remainder of John's Apocalypse.

By asking Christians to conquer by suffering, John's Apocalypse calls upon Christians to be militant (i.e., to stand firmly) without being militaristic. This is a fine line, which takes courage and discernment in equal measure.

Christ as Lamb in the Book of Revelation

This section examines significant passages in the presentation of the Lamb in John's Apocalypse, ending with a brief recap and summary. These are the passages that point to the work of the Lamb and his followers in the face of conflict and adversity.

Worthy Is the Lamb: Revelation 4–5

The vision of the slain Lamb begins in Revelation 4. John receives a vision of God enthroned in heaven, surrounded by his heavenly court (vv. 1-3). The twenty-four elders surround the throne (v. 4). They represent the original twelve patriarchs of the twelve tribes and also the twelve apostles, Jesus's spiritual reconstitution of the tribes. Their white garments symbolize their purity; their crowns, their regal status (see 20:4-6).[22] The theophanic elements of lightning and thunder, coupled with the reference to the seven spirits of God, confirm that the One sitting on the throne is God Almighty (v. 5). "There is no mistaking the significance of such

21. So too Pattemore, *People of God*, 193–212.

22. Cf. John Christopher Thomas and Frank D. Macchia, *Revelation*, THNTC (Grand Rapids: Eerdmans, 2016), 138.

language, for it is standard theophany vocabulary indicating the presence and activity of God. Here, these theophanic elements reveal the awesome presence and power of God proceeding directly from the divine throne."[23] Thomas and Macchia argue that the sea of glass in verse 6a provides a reflection of the glory of God Almighty; however, others argue that it is actually a heavenly version of the Red Sea, seeing a link between Rev 4:6a and 15:2, where Christian saints overcome in both instances.[24]

The next section (4:6b-8) leads to praise of God Almighty by four living creatures. The four creatures represent the four major types of animals on Earth. Each of the creatures has six wings, echoing seraphim in Isaiah 6 and Ezekiel 1, and they praise God without ceasing. This section conveyed to the original readers that the entire creation should praise God at all times. Yet Friesen reminds us,

> John was not content with either [Ezekiel 1 or Isaiah 6], however, and conflated aspects of each to create a new vision distinguishable from the previous two. . . . In this way John simultaneously related his messages to those of two classical prophets and asserted his own authority to relay the messages of God to God's people.[25]

Old images conveying fresh meaning is a motif of John's Apocalypse.

"You Are Worthy!"

The next section (4:9-11) leads to a more significant form of praise. Both the four living creatures and the twenty-four elders praise God Almighty with the words "You are worthy, our Lord and God." When the Roman emperor entered a city, these words went before him, announcing his coming: *dominus et deus noster* (our lord and god). John's vision conveyed to his original audience that such praise rightly and solely belongs to the God of Israel because God is the only Creator who is worthy of glory, honor, and power. As Blount stresses, the emperor "could never credibly claim to have brought into existence the world he so desperately wished

23. Thomas and Macchia, *Revelation*, 139.

24. Thomas and Macchia, *Revelation*, 140; Beale, *Revelation*, 103.

25. Friesen, *Imperial Cults and the Apocalypse*, 174–75.

to control. That prowess is God's alone. Knowing that the ultimate power lies with God, believers ought to feel empowered to resist any claim to lordship tendered by Rome."[26]

Revelation 5 shifts the focus yet again, but not drastically. It introduces the Lamb as the rightful representative of God Almighty: the true God has a true emissary.[27] God Almighty has a scroll in his right hand with seven seals. However, after a thorough search throughout the cosmos, no one is found worthy to open the scroll. And John weeps (vv. 1-4). Unless someone can open the scroll, God's plan for the world cannot come to fruition. An elder comes in verse 5 to console John: "Don't weep. Look! The Lion of the tribe of Judah, the Root of David, has emerged victorious so that he can open the scroll and its seven seals." The "Lion of Judah, the Root of David" represents the expectation of a Davidic Messiah. There is a similar tradition in Isaiah 11, 2 Esdras 11–12, and Sirach 47:22. The Greek word translated "emerged victorious" (*nikao*) can also be translated "has overcome" or "has conquered." In other words, the Lion has thoroughly defeated his opponents, and his victory has made him worthy to open the scroll and sit beside God Almighty. Imperial Roman society would have also viewed the lion as a symbol of power, strength, and victory. For example, there was the story of Hercules wearing the Nemean lion skin, as depicted in the 2014 Dwayne Johnson movie *Hercules.*

The scene shifts rather drastically in the next section (Rev 5:6-10). When John turns, he does not see a Lion, a symbol of military and political prowess, as would have been expected in first-century Roman society. He sees a slain Lamb instead. While the Lamb replaces the Lion for the duration of the Apocalypse, he still manifests images of power. His seven horns connote omnipotence; seven eyes, omniscience. Omnipotence and omniscience are eventually associated with God Almighty.[28] That is why the seven horns and seven eyes represent the seven spirits of God (see 4:5). From this point on, the slain Lamb becomes the major image of Christ in John's Apocalypse. "In 5:5, the angel tells the seer that the Davidic

26. Blount, *Revelation*, 95; cf. Murphy, *Fallen Is Babylon*, 182–87.

27. Cf. J. N. Kraybill, *Imperial Cult and Commerce in John's Apocalypse*, JSNTSup 132 (Sheffield, UK: Sheffield Academic, 1996), 97–98.

28. Thomas and Macchia, *Revelation*, 148; cf. Kraybill, *Cult and Commerce*, 97–99.

messiah will be able to open the scroll. . . . But the form that the messiah takes is a shock," writes Murphy. "But in this life . . . the victory must be won by suffering and death."[29] John's vision would have been incongruent with Greco-Roman triumphalistic expectations.

Grant Osborne writes that the military imagery associated with the Davidic Messiah is very strong throughout the book: "Jesus wages a messianic war against evil and the major weapon that defeats the enemies of God is the cross."[30] Others, like Christopher Rowland, write that the Lion who becomes a Lamb indicates that conquest differs from executing power like a beast.[31]

Kraybill writes, "In John's vision, Jesus confronts the powers of evil, absorbing the worst they can deliver and triumphs over them through resurrection."[32] Blount picks up the mantel: "Without warning, John distances himself from the lion and focuses on what, in terms of strength anyway, is its polar opposite: a Lamb, standing as slaughtered. This is a striking turn of events."[33]

He continues, "John wants his hearers and readers to recognize that Christ's conquest comes by way of his sacrificial, atoning death on the cross."[34] Agreeing, Beale writes, "The slain Lamb represents the image of a conqueror who was mortally wounded while defeating an enemy." He continues, "In John's vision, the Lamb makes a mockery of the prophesied apparent victory of the beast by showing that true power belongs to the One who was slain."[35]

The Lamb is the only one worthy of opening the scroll and setting the divine plan into action. John's original audience would have understood that Jesus's life, death, and resurrection had unexpectedly set these plans into motion. The Lamb takes the scroll (v. 7). The four living creatures

29. Murphy, *Fallen Is Babylon*, 193; cf. Kraybill, *Cult and Commerce*, 97–98.

30. Osborne, *Revelation*, 254; cf. Blount, *Revelation*, 105–6.

31. Christopher Rowland, "Revelation," *NIB* 12:576; see also Koester, *Revelation*, 375–76.

32. Kraybill, *Cult and Commerce*, 101. Also see the more complete discussion (100–102).

33. Blount, *Revelation*, 108.

34. Blount, *Revelation*, 109.

35. Beale, *Revelation*, 114.

and twenty-four elders show reverence for the Lamb and sing a new song (v. 8). The song states that the Lamb is worthy to open the scroll because

> you were slain,
> and by your blood you purchased for God
> persons from every tribe, language, people and nation. (v. 9)

As a result, those redeemed by the Lamb constitute a kingdom of priests, persons who may dare to approach God Almighty (see Rev 21:1-7, 22-26). This new song echoes the hymn in 4:11 in that both begin with the words "You are worthy." This is a principal theme in the vision, associating attributes normally given to God Almighty with the Christ. This hymn also states why the Lamb was worthy and what benefactions for his followers his sacrifice has accomplished.[36]

The last segment (5:11-14) reiterates and expands upon the two previous hymns in Revelation 4:11 and 5:9-10. Millions of angels join the four living creatures and twenty-four elders in praise. This hymn states that the slaughtered Lamb is worthy to receive power, wealth, wisdom, might, honor, glory, and blessing, attributes and praise normally associated with God Almighty (cf. 1 Chr 29:11-12). This segment ends with a hymn of praise jointly to God Almighty and the Lamb by the entire universe. The four living creatures say "Amen," connoting that those closest to God confirm the appropriateness of the praise.[37] The twenty-four elders connoted the same thing by falling down in worship.

In Revelation 4–5, one finds two significant transformations. The first is the transformation of the messianic Lion into a slain Lamb. Based upon the historical reality of the crucifixion of Jesus, this transformation would not only have been unexpected among Jews, it would have been unexpected by most people in Roman imperial society. The second transformation follows the first: conquering, or "emerging victorious," is no longer done through military or political means but through suffering. This change would have been as unexpected as the first. Throughout the

36. Cf. Kraybill, *Cult and Commerce*, 100–102; see also Blount's discussion of the hymns of Revelation as songs of resistance (*Revelation*, 95–98). See also Koester, *Revelation*, 379–81.

37. Cf. Murphy, *Fallen Is Babylon*, 198–99.

remainder of the book, victory/overcoming/conquering comes through bearing a faithful witness, not fighting, "even unto death" (Rev 12:11, author translation). John expresses bearing witness in military terms in order to convey the difficulty of witnessing under duress (cf. Eph 6:7-10) and also because it is a perennial feature of Jewish apocalypticism (e.g., 1 En. 10; 2 Esd 11–13). At no point do the warriors in 14:1-5 or 19:11-21 ever engage in battle. They conquered through their witness and thus sit on thrones in 20:4-6. No passage in Revelation demonstrates this more clearly than 12:7-12, our next segment.

Divine Punishment

And the Lord said to Gabriel, "Proceed against the bastards and the reprobates and against the sons of the fornicators, and destroy the sons of the fornicators and the sons of the Watchers from amongst men. And send them out, and send them against one another, and let them destroy themselves in battle, for they will not have length of days." (1 En. 10:9)[38]

Opening the Seven Seals

The Christ-Lamb comes and inaugurates the eschatological woes. This is a prophetic act because the scroll contains an account of the eschatological events to bring human history to completion. This all occurs in heaven, but the intended audience would have understood that what occurred in heaven must be repeated on Earth. For example, Revelation 12:7-12 is a heavenly vision of what will occur on earth in 19:11-21, which in turn is a precursor of 20:7-10. In this instance, the Lamb functions as a revealer.

The first four seals bring about the eschatological woes common to Jewish apocalypticism (e.g., 2 Bar. 27 and 53). The horse of different colors is the primary referent with the opening of each seal. Each seal brings suffering, especially the types of suffering common to the exodus narrative.

The fifth seal (6:9-11) brings something of an interlude from the end-time suffering. Rather, it refers to a specific type of suffering, the suffering of the Christian martyrs. They have given their lives for the faith, "those who had been slaughtered on account of the word of God and the witness they had given" (6:9). They ask how long will their deaths go unavenged,

38. Knibb, "1 Enoch."

a question of theodicy found in other apocalypses (e.g., 1 En. 47:4; 2 Esd 4:33-37; 2 Bar. 23:4-5). This is a very human question. People who have suffered unjustly still want justice even if they want it in silence. This question comes from a community in distress not because they have committed crimes, but because they have kept the faith and not denied it even under duress.

Heroic Resistance

John McCain, the late US senator from Arizona, was an American war hero who endured several years as a prisoner of the North Vietnamese during the Vietnam War. He suffered physical and mental abuse, malnutrition and other indignities, and did not betray his country. He kept the faith and found a way of being militant although he could not physically fight back. All who have endured such inhumane treatment are heroes. They are a testament of the power of the human spirit to persevere against all odds.

The sixth seal shifts the scene yet again (6:12-17). These verses can be divided into two parts. In verses 12-14, we have another vision of the eschatological woes: an earthquake, a solar eclipse, a lunar eclipse, a falling star, a receding sky, and the dislodging of every mountain and island. These are signs to the informed reader that the end is near. Jewish and early Christian literature have many such examples (e.g., Isa 13:10; Hag 2:6-7; Sib. Or. 3:75-92; 2 Bar. 70:8; 2 Esd 5:8; Mark 13:24-25; 2 Pet 3:11-12). In the second scene (vv. 15-17), the kings, the upper class, the generals, the rich, the strong, every slave and freedman have hidden themselves because they have recognized the end-of-time signs and attempted to avoid the wrath of the Lamb. In most instances in the Hebrew Bible and Second Temple Judaism, God alone causes the end time to come. The Messiah is merely an agent of God in the process (e.g., 2 Esd 11–13). In Revelation, however, the Christ-Lamb joins God Almighty as an associate, that is, God shares the divine role with the Messiah. It is noteworthy, however, that the martyrs who often accompany Christ never engage the enemy in battle (e.g. Rev 14:1-5; 19:11-21).

The opening of the seventh seal brings another shift in the narrative (Rev 7:9–8:1). An innumerable, culturally diverse eschatological

Christian community stands before the heavenly coregents. They wear white garments and receive palm branches, both emblematic of their religious propriety and salvific victory (cf. 1 Macc 13:51). This is the same group envisioned in Revelation 6:9-11 who also receive white garments. They will reappear in 14:1-5.

Revelation 7:9-17 builds upon 6:9-11 by adding that God's care for the saints and God's punishment of evildoers are parts of God's plan: "These are the ones who have come out of the great tribulation and washed their robes and made them white by means of the blood of the Lamb" (Rev 7:14, author translation). They take positions of esteem before the throne of God and worship God continuously. They no longer suffer from physical needs or from sudden changes in the natural environment "because the Lamb . . . will shepherd them." He will lead them to the springs of life-giving water, "and God will wipe away every tear from their eyes" (7:17). This is a prelude to the events to come found in more detail in Revelation 21:1-7. This vision of praise in heaven would have been a powerful word of assurance to those suffering under regional repression in Roman Asia.

The sequence rightly ends with silence in heaven (8:1). Each morning the high priest entered the temple in Jerusalem, reflecting a tradition found in the *Testament of Adam* 1:12 (cf. 1 En. 47:1-2; Tob. 12:15). It parallels in heaven what occurred each morning when the high priest prayed for the Jewish people throughout the world. He burned incense, and as the smoke went skyward it symbolized the ascent of the prayers of the people to heaven. This took about thirty minutes. This vision of silence in heaven probably communicated to Asian Christians that their prayers had been heard and answered in 7:14-17.[39]

War in Heaven: Revelation 12:7-12

Revelation 12:7-12 provides the second significant text. This passage begins with war breaking out in heaven between the archangel Michael

39. Richard Bauckham, *The Climax of Prophecy: Studies in the Book of Revelation* (Edinburgh: T&T Clark, 1993), 70–83. Koester notes that silence during times of prayer would have been the norm in Greco-Roman contexts as well "since silence showed reverence when a leader offered prayers" (*Revelation*, 434).

and his angels, on one side, and Satan and his angels, on the other.[40] Michael and his entourage defeat Satan and his entourage and the latter group is cast from heaven (vv. 8-9). The vision concludes with a hymn celebrating the victory in heaven but a lament over the eschatological woes coming to earth (vv. 10-12).

The hymn in Revelation 12:10-12 requires a closer look. Michael functions as a heavenly divine warrior, God's divine eschatological agent, but Michael's victory is not his own. It belongs to Christ. Michael and his angels have "gained the victory" over Satan and his angels "on account of the blood of the Lamb and the word of their witness." Revelation 12:10-11 has an unexpected message in two distinct ways. First, persons in the ancient world expected events in the heavens to lead to parallel events on Earth. However, Christ's victory on earth has led to Michael's victory in heaven. This is a reversal of expectations. This reversal is in keeping with the Lamb replacing the Lion and suffering as the vehicle of this conquest. Additionally, the Greek word *nikao* has been translated "gained the victory." It is the same verb found in 5:5 ("emerged victorious") and connotes that the Lamb has conquered through faithfulness and not weapons. Victory in Revelation 12:1-11 has come through the Lamb's suffering and not through actual combat. Victory in Revelation 12:10-11 comes by means of a strong witness.[41]

The Archangel Michael

And these are the names of the holy angels who watch: Michael, one of the holy angels, for (he is) obedient in his benevolence over the people and the nations. (1 En. 20:1, 5)[42]

Revelation 12:11 echoes 5:9 in a significant way. Revelation 5:9 reads, "And they sang a new song, saying, 'You are worthy to receive the scroll and to open its seals because you were slain and you redeemed to God

40. Michael is Israel's patron angel in many Second Temple Jewish writings (e.g., Dan 10:13-21 and 12:1; 1 En. 20; *1QM* 13:10; 17:7-8; cf. *T. Dan* 6:2; *T. Levi* 5:5-6).

41. Cf. Koester, *Revelation*, 563–65.

42. E. Isaac, trans., "1 (Ethiopic Apocalypse of) Enoch, *OTP*, vol. 1.

through your blood persons from every tribe, language, people and nation'" (author translation; italics added). Similarly, Revelation 12:11 reads, "And they *conquered* [*nikao*] him through the blood of the Lamb and through the word of their witness" (author translation). Revelation 12:11 complements 5:9 by telling the original audience how the Lamb has conquered in heaven. This is an example in John's Apocalypse where later visions build upon earlier ones. Additionally, "the blood of the Lamb" and "the word of their witness" are complementary parallels in that they define each other. Christ's death derived from Christ's faithful witness "even unto death." Thus, early Christianity's faithful witness to Christ leads to the community's suffering. In turn, this same witness leads to their victory and their exoneration.

The blood of the Lamb and the witness of the saints are the means by which evil is defeated in heaven by Christ and also on Earth by the Christian community. In neither instance is there actual combat. Moreover, "the blood of the Lamb" and "the word of their witness" are parallel statements, followed by a third parallel: "and they loved not their lives even unto death" (author translation). Victory has been redefined by the Christ event: victory comes through suffering or a willingness to suffer for one's religious convictions. Conquest does not require military action but religious fidelity.[43]

A Sacrificial Hymn

Who defeats my fiercest foes?
Who consoles my saddest woes?
Who revives my fainting heart,
healing all its hidden smart?
Jesus Christ, the crucified.

—Hymn, "Ask Ye What Great Thing I Know," verse 2

43. See also Osborne, *Revelation*, 473–80; Murphy, *Fallen Is Babylon*, 286–92; Beale, *Revelation: Shorter*, 252–59; Blount, *Revelation*, 235–39.

The Two Beasts: Revelation 13:8, 11

Revelation 13:8 is a hinge in verses 1-10, the vision of the first of two beasts. The beast in 13:8 ascends from the sea and has ten horns, symbols of power, and ten diadems on seven heads, symbols of its royal authority. This verse refers to the names written in the Lamb's scroll of life before creation itself (see Rev 3:5; 17:8; 20:12; 21:27). The Lamb has prerecorded the names of those who shall live in the New Jerusalem, conveying to Asian Christians that their places are assured in spite of their suffering.

Revelation 13:11 details the second beast from the land who looks like a lamb. This beast is neither a lamb nor a dragon but has characteristics of those animals, forming a contrast between the true Lamb of God and his opposite. Koester reminds us that "readers are to see the beast as the demonic counterpart to the Lamb. The Lamb's power is not merely greater than that of the beast, it is different in kind."[44]

This passage would have said to Asian Christians that at the end of time Satan would appear to be the Messiah, but he was actually a dragon. This beast has not come to save the world but to exploit it. He represents the power of local Roman authorities in charge of the local imperial cult.[45] The visions of the two beasts in Revelation 13 would have resonated with the massive power of the Roman Empire to control its subjects both globally and locally. However, the first-century Christians living in Asia would have taken away assurance that victory was decided before the acts of creation commenced. This blessed assurance is encouraging for anyone experiencing subjugation and oppression.

An Army in Heaven: Revelation 14:1-5

Revelation 14:1-5 is a vision of the heavenly Mount Zion. This passage is an eschatological exodus vision set in heaven. The prowess of the heavenly forces is unimpeachable. First, Mount Zion symbolized the place of deliverance (e.g., Ps 2:6-7; 2 Esd 13:34-38; see also Rev 21:9–22:5). Further, the number 144,000 symbolizes the perfect Israel, a select group that has secret knowledge (the new song in v. 3). In addition, they have

44. Koester, *Revelation*, 577.

45. Simon Price, *Rituals and Power: The Roman Imperial Cult in Asia Minor* (Cambridge: Cambridge University Press, 1984), 197–98; Koester, *Revelation*, 576–79.

been redeemed as first-fruits dedicated as a tithe to God and the Lamb: they are the best of the best (e.g., Exod 23:19; Neh 10:35; Prov 3:9; Rom 8:23; 1 Cor 15:20-23; cf. Rom 11:16; 2 Cor 1:22; 5:5; Eph 1:13-14). They are virgins, in that context symbolizing their moral purity. Blount suggests that "first-fruits" points to the expectation that other fruits will soon follow the very best and inspire Asian Christians to remain strong in their faith.[46]

Second, the 144,000 constitutes a righteous religious army prepared for holy war.[47] During conflict, Israelite soldiers were required to abstain from sexual intercourse (see 1 Sam 21:4-5; 2 Sam 11:11; see also Exod 19:14-15). Revelation 14:1-5 parallels 7:1-8 and both passages refer to emblems on the saints that set them apart (7:3 and 14:1). Both recount the deliverance of the saints from the great tribulation (7:15-17; 14:3). Finally, both passages relate how the saints have faithfully followed the Christ-Lamb and even have given their lives for their religious convictions (7:14; 14:4).[48] In neither passage do the saints actually engage in battle.[49] And the followers of the Lamb emulate the Lamb, even if it means their death, the very means of defeating evil.[50]

In Revelation 14:1-5, the Lamb gathers to himself a select community of saints whose discipleship, fidelity, and morality are unquestionable and beyond reproach. Instead of suggesting Christian accommodation or religious laxity, this military imagery communicated how hostile the environment was for Christians and the need for religious purity and a deep faith to withstand social pressures.

Eternal Punishment of the Wicked: Revelation 14:10

Revelation 14:10 relates the eternal torment awaiting the beast and his followers: "they themselves will also drink the wine of God's passionate

46. Blount, *Revelation*, 268–70. Cf. Thomas and Macchia, *Revelation*, 253–54.

47. See G. B. Caird, *A Commentary on the Revelation of St. John the Divine*, HNTC (New York/Evanston: Harper & Row, 1966), 177–81.

48. Cf. Aune, *Revelation*, 2:794–96.

49. Rev 19:11-21 continues the victories mentioned in Rev 7:8-8:1; 12:7-12; 14:1-5. Christians do not engage in battle in 19:11-21 either.

50. Thomas and Macchia, *Revelation*, 250–56.

anger, poured full strength into the cup of his wrath. They will suffer the pain of fire and sulfur in the presence of the holy angels and the Lamb." "The holy angels" could be a pious reference to God Almighty or to the divine assembly around the throne of the Lamb. If this were indeed the case, both God and the Lamb would view the punishment of the oppressors of the martyrs. On the other hand, the passage could mean exactly what it says. In either case, the Lamb witnesses[51] the punishment of those who killed him and oppressed his followers. Just as the martyrs suffered publicly on Earth, the beast and his cohort shall suffer publicly in heaven. Indeed, those who opposed the Lamb on Earth would see him observing their eternal demise and recognize too late their mistake and his righteousness.[52] This vision depicts the ultimate vindication of Asian Christians who have been suppressed for their lack of participation in the ruler cult in that region. The martyrs do not punish the beast and his followers. God alone does that. That is why the martyrs ask God in 6:9-11 when God will act.[53]

The Song of Moses and the Lamb: Revelation 15:3-4

These verses fall within the vision of the angels with the last plagues (15:1-8). The Song of Moses and the Lamb celebrates God's eschatological exodus of his people. This song is similar to the Song of Moses in Exodus 15. Both songs are sung along a seashore. Mentioning both Moses and the Lamb connects the first people of God with the new people of God in the same way that Revelation 7 relates the first people of God, the early identified Jewish Christians as a perfect (complete) community of 144,000 from the twelve tribes of Israel, to the new people of God who are multicultural and international. The first community is exclusive, reflecting the uniqueness of Israel among the nations; the second, inclusive and reflecting more the perspective of Diaspora Judaism in the first century. Finally, both Moses and the Lamb function as deliverers of a religious body, again connecting the past and the present (cf. Eph 2).

51. Yes, this is a play on words.

52. Cf. J. Ellul, *Apocalypse* (New York: Seabury, 1977), 176.

53. Cf. Koester on symmetry and divine judgment (*Revelation*, 621–22).

The Fall of the Great Prostitute: Revelation 17:1-14

In Revelation, which of course is steeped in patriarchal imagination, John sees a vision of the great prostitute (17:1). References to sexual immorality and substance abuse are metaphors for the prostitute's sinfulness (v. 2) and the repression of Christians (v. 6). The prostitute receives the name "Babylon the great," a symbolic reference to Rome and its rulers (see v. 9).[54] The Roman Empire will engage the Lamb in battle, but the Lamb shall conquer (*nikao*) them because "he is Lord of lords and King of kings. Those with him are called, chosen, and faithful" (v. 14).

"Babylon," the Evil Empire

He will flee from Babylon, a terrible and shameless prince, whom all mortals and noble men despise. (*Sib. Or.* 5:143-44)[55]

The victory over evil has already been won by the Lamb. The role of Asian Christians is to remain faithful, even in times of tribulation. These tribulations are in the future (as the tense of the verbs make clear). So Revelation 17:14 is a prophecy that gives instructions to Christians on how they should act during the coming crisis. At no point does John envision Christians taking up arms. The modus vivendi is not fighting but witnessing faithfully "to the word of God and the witness of Christ Jesus," that is, emerging victorious through their testimony in word and action as did Christ Jesus.

The "called, chosen, and faithful" connoted to the original readers that Asian Christians had an elite status. The coming battle will occur in the future, but the vision itself will not be realized until Revelation 19:11-21. Indeed, both 17:14 and 19:16 refer to the Messiah as "Lord of lords and King of kings." More important, Revelation 17:14 provides a word of assurance for the Christian community: the followers of the Lamb are called and chosen, terms denoting the election of Israel as the people of God, and faithful, an exhortation to remain vigilant to God's word. The

54. *Babylon* is a code name for Rome in *Sib. Or.* 5:144; 1 Pet 5:13; 2 Esd 1:1.

55. J. J. Collins, trans., "Sibylline Oracles," *OTP*, vol. 1.

military language is not used as a call to arms but as a means to convey the difficulty of the task before Christians and the need to remain faithful throughout the ordeal. Furthermore, those three adjectives serve important roles for the emotional well-being of the seven churches. The first two connote strong deterministic elements; in other words, they say that Asian Christians have a unique relationship to God Almighty, which assures them of their ultimate salvation, even in the face of intense repression. This is a recurring theme in Revelation (e.g., 1:5-6; 3:5; 6:9; 12:10-11; 14:1-5; 17:8; 20:4-6). "Faithful" denotes that the saints must remain true to their calling and election. Collectively, the three terms tell us that Asian Christians saw themselves as special persons enduring an unjust ordeal, but they are assured that God Almighty will reward their faithfulness in a special way. God cares for the most faithful followers of the Lamb because they need it the most (17:1-6).

This passage reflects a social setting where the faithfulness of Christians, that is their discipleship practices modeled on the faithfulness of Christ all the way to the cross, has led to their suffering. This faithful witness is also their means of attaining ultimate victory. Within this type of context, the selection of the predicates "called," "elect," and "faithful" are intelligible as both exhortation and apologetics. As exhortation, they encourage the readers to believe that their faithfulness in following Jesus is the proper response to oppression and will ultimately lead to their salvation and vindication. As apologetics, it explains to the Christians that their suffering is not a sign of their sinfulness but a sign of their piety and righteousness. In Revelation, righteousness leads to the suppression of the righteous and the best weapon against it is remaining faithful. They must leave ultimate vindication to God Almighty. One finds similar sentiments in Matthew 25:31-46, Galatians 5:6, James 2:14-17, and 1 Peter 1:11-23.

The Wedding Supper: Revelation 19:7-9

Revelation 19:7-9 falls within the vision of the Lamb's wedding supper, or wedding banquet (19:5-10). The bride is a more positive female image than the prostitute in Revelation 17:1-14. The bride of the Lamb is the community of Christian saints. This would have communicated the closeness of the community to her Lord, similar to the close covenant relationship within a marriage. This would have reinforced the recurring concept in Revelation that there is no separation between God Almighty and Christ, on the divine side of the equation, and the earthly Christian community, on the human side (e.g., 1:9; 6:9; 20:4; cf. Eph 5:25-30). The fidelity of the community's witness to Christ must match the fidelity of Christ's witness to God: there is an unbroken chain between Almighty God, Christ, and the Christian community with Christ as the fundamental link that holds it all together (cf. Eph 2:20-22).

Revelation 19:8 refers to the wedding garment as "pure, bright, fine linen [Greek: *bussinon*]; for the fine linen is the righteous deeds of the saints" (author translation). Bright, radiant linen had established roles symbolizing purity, and such attire was worn most often by heavenly beings and priests in the Hebrew Bible and Jewish writings into the second century CE (e.g., Lev 16:4; Ezek 9:2-3; Dan 10:5-6; 1 En. 62:15-16; 2 Bar. 51:5; Philo, *Mos.* 2.17; Josephus, *J. W.* 5.230-37; *Apoc. Ab.* 13:15). Philo and Josephus describe the high priest's attire with the same Greek word found in Revelation 19:8 (*bussinos*). Revelation 15:6 describes angels similarly as "clothed in pure bright [*katharon lampron*] linen" and Revelation 19:14 uses similar terms to describe the attire of the saints who accompany the Divine Warrior (*bussinon*). In all these instances, linen connoted purity. In this prophetic vision, John sees an undefiled church entering into a new era (cf. 7:13-14; 14:1; 20:4-6). This vision presupposes that the churches of Asia have followed the example and the instructions of their Lord in Revelation 2:1–3:22, and are thoroughly prepared to enter the New Jerusalem. They have borne faithful witnesses and have "emerged victorious" (2:7). Revelation 19:9 concludes with a word of assurance by an angel: "These are the true words of God." In other words, this is a "done deal."

The New Jerusalem: Revelation 21–22

This last vision describes the New Jerusalem more completely than any other section of the book and mentions the Lamb six times (21:14,

22, 23, 27; 22:1, 3). The Lamb plays a key role in securing and maintaining the spiritual and physical well-being of the Christian community.

Revelation 21:14 connects the ministry of the historical Jesus with the christological Lamb of Revelation by referring to the twelve foundations of the New Jerusalem with "the twelve names of the Lamb's twelve apostles." This follows the reference to the twelve tribes in 21:12. Making this connection conveyed to the original audience that the Christian faith community is embedded in and extends the faith of Israel. Moreover, connecting the Lamb with Jesus cements the Lamb as the central christological image in the Apocalypse. This connection makes the community gathered in Jesus's name the most faithful expression of Judaism for John and the faithful he addresses.

Revelation 21:27 states that "only those who are registered in the Lamb's scroll of life" shall enter the New Jerusalem. This passage conveyed to Asian Christians an assurance of their entry into the new city in the new era, no matter what suffering they are facing.

Revelation 21:22-23 and 22:1, 3 must be discussed together because all four verses present the Lamb as God Almighty's vice regent. This relationship between these two figures has been noted several times previously in this study. Moreover, all four passages relate Christ to the community's life in the New Jerusalem. These two factors tell the reader that God Almighty and Christ are concerned deeply with the quality of life in the present as well as the coming new age. Moreover, it strongly suggests that the quality of life on Earth for Christians has been poor. It also discloses to the reader the Lamb's concern for the well-being of the community, a link between Christ and community.

The New Jerusalem has no temple, because God Almighty and the Lamb are its temple (21:22). This is a reversal of expectations given in the vision of Ezekiel 40–46. Instead of only the high priest having direct access to God, all the inhabitants of the New Jerusalem are priests (1:6) and have access to God. The city also does not have heavenly luminaries for God and the Lamb illuminate it. These two verses signify that the temple was no longer necessary because the divine coregents shall dwell among humankind and become the center of life for the community.[56]

Revelation 22:1-5 confirms the preceding comments. The river of the water of life flows from the throne of God and the Lamb (21:1). The river provides nourishment for the tree of life, which in turn heals the nations (21:2; cf. 21:27). Only the pure will enter the city and the throne of God and the Lamb will be in it (v. 3). Verse 4 contains the key element: "They will see [God's] face, and his name will be on their foreheads," that is, they will be priests (see 1:5; 5:9) and God's emblem shall be on them, designating their election and separating them from the unjust (see 3:12; 7:3; 14:1). Verse 5 reiterates 21:23. These verses provide yet another example of the Lamb's providential oversight of the Christian community.

In sum, the New Jerusalem will be the eschatological home for God, the Lamb, and their faithful followers. The eschatological exodus ends in the New Jerusalem.[57] The New Jerusalem will establish an intimate, familial relation among God, the Lamb, and their followers. A symbol of this intimacy is the reference to the priestly nature of the elect in the eschatological community, which will have direct access to God and the Lamb. This reinforces the wedding imagery in 19:5-9. God and the Lamb, in turn, will provide the highest quality of life possible and the servants of God will worship them (22:5; cf. 7:14-17). The New Jerusalem will be a community full of happiness and free of disease, founded by God and the Lamb. The reference to healing the nations might be a message of solace to Asian Christians since Genesis 2:9 makes no mention of healing. Many have suffered (Rev 6:9-11; 20:4-6). This passage has several eschatological exodus images in the office of priest, the end of the exodus, the New Jerusalem, and the election of the New Israel.

This chapter examined the Christology of John's Apocalypse. It demonstrates that the slain Lamb is the major image of Christ in the book. Revelation 5:5-6 is the key passage. In these two verses, John is told the Lion of Judah, a symbol for the Davidic Messiah, has conquered (*nikao*) and is worthy to open the scroll; however, when John turns he sees a slain

56. Cf. Caird, *St. John the Divine*, 278–79; Blount, *Revelation*, 392–93.

57. See Bauckham, *Theology*, 70–72.

Lamb instead. From this point on, the term *nikao* clearly refers to a victory through suffering. This victory required an unwavering witness. As with Christ, it could lead to death. When this witness occurred before Roman officials or provincial leaders in service to the imperial cult, this witness became a form of civil disobedience. Thus, within this context, just as the slain Lamb has replaced the Lion of Judah, witnessing faithfully even unto death has replaced making war for the Apocalypse. These two transformations, from Lion to Lamb and from making war to bearing witness, shall lead to a third transformation, the transformation of *marturia* from witnessing in court to witnessing fervently even if it means dying for one's beliefs.

Study Questions

1. How has the life of the historical Jesus impacted the concept of Christ in John's Apocalypse?
2. What about this chapter has surprised you the most?
3. How has John's use of traditional imagery been changed?
4. Can you understand how John's concept of Christ would have seemed silly to non-Christians but edifying for Christians?
5. Where is the end of the new exodus for John's Apocalypse?
6. Can you give an example of how John's images of Christ are consistent?

Chapter 3

BEARING WITNESS

The Greek word *nikao* meant to be victorious, to conquer; to win (a legal case); to vanquish, to overcome. *Nike* meant victory.[1] This section of chapter 3 shall demonstrate how John transformed the meaning of *nikao* and its cognate forms to mean victory through suffering for Christians. The passion, crucifixion, and resurrection of Christ served as John's models. Asian Christians must remain faithful and wait upon God for the victory. On the other hand, where victory comes through the use of power, that power is evil and the victory is short-lived.

The second section of chapter 3 examines the Christ as the Divine Warrior (DW) in Revelation 19:11-21. This section will show links with other major images of Christ in John's Apocalypse, demonstrating both the internal unity of the work as a whole and also the theological consistency of the work as a whole. Even as DW, Christ conquers by means of a faithful, spoken witness.

The Transformation of *Nikao* and *Nike*

We turn now to an examination of the word *nikao* in Revelation 2–3. While these passages do not refer to the Lamb, they do demonstrate the

1. Cf. W. Bauer, *A Greek-English Lexicon of the New Testament and Other Early Christian Literature*, trans. W. F. Arndt and F. W. Gingrich (Chicago: University of Chicago Press, 1979), 539. Cf. Grant R. Osborne, *Revelation*, BECNT (Grand Rapids: Baker Academic, 2002), 122; Craig R. Koester, *Revelation: A New Translation with Introduction and Commentary*, AB (New Haven, CT: Yale University Press, 2014), 265.

christological consistency among the visions as well as maintaining a victory through suffering motif.

Nikao is found fifteen times in the Book of Revelation (2:7, 11, 17, 26; 3:5, 12, 21; 5:5; 6:2; 11:7; 12:11; 13:7; 15:2; 17:14; 21:7).[2] The first seven occurrences are found in the seven messages in Revelation 2–3 (see comments below). Revelation 5:5, 12:11, and 17:14 have been discussed in the previous chapter. This chapter will discuss the term in Revelation 2–3, 6:2; 11:7; 13:7; 15:2; and 21:7. Murphy writes, "The promises at the end of each message in Revelation 2–3 tie the messages to the eschatological fulfillment in Revelation 20–22."[3] In agreement, Beale writes, "Although the promises are phrased differently in each letter, they are all versions of the final promise of the book," which is "the enjoyment of God's covenantal presence among his people."[4]

Our discussion will demonstrate a distinctive difference between the use of the term when it is associated with Christians and when it is associated with non-Christians. Just as John has transformed the meaning of *martus* from giving a legal testimony to dying for one's faith, John has transformed *nikao* and its cognates from a political, athletic, or legal victory to victory through suffering.[5] Indeed, the CEB translates *nikao* as "to emerge victorious." This rendering is sensitive to the manner in which John has changed its meaning. An examination of the use of the term in the seven messages to the churches in Revelation 2–3 will help to demonstrate what brings victory to Christians.

Ephesus

In this letter Christ notes the good and the bad in Ephesus and encourages them to increase in the good or Christ "will move your lampstand from its place" (2:5). The promises to the victors follow.

2. See, e.g., Christopher Rowland, *NIB* 12:576; Osborne, *Revelation*, 122.

3. F. J. Murphy, *Fallen Is Babylon: The Revelation to John* (Harrisburg, PA: Trinity, 1998), 118.

4. G. K. Beale, *Revelation: A Shorter Commentary*, with David H. Campbell (Grand Rapids: Eerdmans, 2015), 59.

5. O. Bauernfeind, "*Nikao*," in G. Kittle, ed., *Theological Dictionary of the New Testament*, 10 vols., G. W. Bromiley, trans. (Grand Rapids: Eerdmans, 1967), 4:942–45. Clearly someone at Nike, Inc. has a classical education.

Christ declares, "I will allow those who emerge victorious [*nikonti*] to eat from the tree of life, which is in God's paradise" (2:7; see 22:2, 14).[6] Revelation 22:14 states that those who wash their robes have a right to the healing powers of the tree of life in the New Jerusalem. Washing their robes relates to 7:14, where the ones who have washed their robes in the blood of the Lamb shall be protected and made whole by God in the New Jerusalem. The washing of their robes in the blood of the Lamb represents their giving of their lives as Christ gave his life and also attaining victory as Christ attained victory through suffering. At once, the reader learns the stringent demands of Christian discipleship and also the reader receives surety that the benefits outweigh the dangers.

Beale writes, "Believers must obey the exhortation to persevere and remain faithful if they wish to be heirs of the divine promise."[7] Echoing Beale, Blount writes, "To conquer is to witness resistantly." Blount quickly adds that this does not mean that the conqueror has won. He observes that Jesus, John, and Antipas all have suffered because of their fidelity to God. It does mean that "like Christ, through the very act of witnessing," Christians will "overwhelm the bestial forces of draconian Rome and obtain eschatological relationship with God."[8] Christians must overcome by bearing witness, not by bearing arms. They must be militant by being firm in their faithfulness, not by being militaristic. Conquering "is also used in a transferred sense for the Lamb and his followers, who bear witness even at the cost of their lives."[9]

Victory outside the Apocalypse

"When passion has won [*nikese*] an evil victory [*niken*], mind gives in, being prevented from giving heed to itself and to all its own occupations." (Philo, *Allegorical Interpretation* 3.186)[10]

6. The object of the sentence in Greek is in the singular: "I will allow the *one who* emerges victorious. . . ."

7. Beale, *Revelation*, 59; cf. Murphy, *Fallen Is Babylon*, 117–18.

8. B. K. Blount, *Revelation: A Commentary*, NTL (Louisville: Westminster John Knox, 2009), 52.

9. Koester, *Revelation*, 271.

10. Loeb Classical Library translation.

Smyrna

The congregation in Smyrna has been under great duress, but it has sustained its faith. This community receives no condemnation, only commendation.

The message to Smyrna gives two promises. "Be faithful even to the point of death, and I will give you the crown [*stephanos*] of life" (2:10), a prime example of the victory through suffering motif. One finds a second promise in 2:11: "Those who emerge victorious [*nikon*] won't be hurt by the second death."[11] These two promises must be understood together. The *stephanos* was customarily awarded to winners at athletic games. It is to be contrasted with the *diadema*, which denoted royalty. Christians then would be victorious in life and gain eternal life at the judgment if they remain faithful. This promise is not explicitly fulfilled in Revelation, but the second promise, avoiding the second death, is fulfilled explicitly (see 20:6, 14; 21:8). Thus, the first promise is another version of the second.

The second promise guarantees that the faithful will escape the second death and thereby be resurrected to life eternal, enabling them to avoid the second death. Indeed, given the double negative in 2:11 (*ou me*), "won't" is a good translation, but it might be better to render it, "Those who emerge victorious *shall never* be hurt by the second death."[12] Victory comes not through military means but through maintaining a faithful witness, even if it means death (2:10).[13]

The lake of fire is the second death (21:8). The second death conveyed complete, eternal separation from God Almighty. It is the opposite of receiving the crown of life and eating from the tree of life. This concept was widespread in Second Temple Judaism (e.g., 1 En. 69:27-29; *IQS* 4.2-14; 2 Esd 7:32-44; 2 Bar. 54.15-22).

---

11. Again, the Greek reads, "the one who."

12. While double negatives are not good grammar in English, they are perfectly fine in Greek, where they functioned to convey the author's belief that something certainly would not occur.

13. Cf. Ben Witherington III, *Revelation,* NCBC (New York: Cambridge University Press, 2003), 98–101; Koester, *Revelation*, 278–82.

Eternal Punishment

And I looked...and I saw there a deep valley with burning fire. And they brought the kings and the powerful and threw them into that valley. (1 En. 54:1-2)[14]

Pergamum

Christians in Pergamum receive a mixed message. On the one hand, they are commended for remaining faithful to the name even under duress and after the killing of Antipas, "my faithful witness"; however, they are severely chastised because some participate in the Balaam movement and some also follow the Nicolaitans. The references to improper sexual behavior may be literal or metaphors for unfaithfulness and involvement in the two other movements.[15]

The promise in the message to Pergamum is threefold: (1) the hidden manna; (2) a white stone with new name; (3) a name no one knows except its recipient (2:17). The hidden manna tradition asserted that Jeremiah had taken the manna from the temple and that it would reappear during the messianic age (2 Macc 2:4-8). It is probably this tradition to which this passage refers. The white stone connoted purity, righteousness, holiness, and similar virtues. The new name and the name no one knows are probably one and the same. It also echoes the mystery religions, where only the saved have certain knowledge. Thus, only Asian Christians knew that the apparent victims were actually the victors. This name saves the ones who receive it.

The new name has very positive connotations in John's Apocalypse. "New" (*kainos*) connotes in the Apocalypse an improved, righteous quality of life. It communicated righteousness, holiness, and election. For example, the four living creatures and the twenty-four elders sing a new song with the appearance of the Lamb (5:9); the 144,000 martyrs on Mount Zion also sing a new song (14:3), and the culmination of the Apocalypse has the new heaven and the new earth (21:1-5).

14. M. A. Knibb translation, *AOT*.

15. I discuss this in more detail in *Christ and Community: A Socio Historical Study of the Christology of Revelation*, JSNTSup (Sheffield, UK: Sheffield Academic Press, 1999), 124–32.

The new name is God's name and also Christ's name. God Almighty and Christ are inseparable in Revelation (see 1:8 on God Almighty and 1:17c; also 2:28). The new name is most probably "Christian."[16] Christians have taken a name that was probably a derogatory reference to them and turned a negative into a positive. Ironically, outsiders do not know this new name is actually a good thing. The true victor must claim the name.[17]

Embracing the Methodist Slur

The early followers of John Wesley were mocked with the name *Methodist.* So they embraced the slur and made it the name of their approach to Christian discipleship. In a similar way, *Obamacare* began as a negative label from Republicans for the Affordable Care Act. President Barack Obama embraced the name and took much of the sting out of the insult.

Thyatira

The message to Thyatira follows a familiar pattern of first giving commendations and then corrective instructions. The community has done some good things, but it has "put up" with Jezebel, most probably a symbolic name for the leader of a rival prophetic movement.

Authority over the nations and the morning star are the two promises to those who "emerge victorious" in Thyatira (2:26-28). They must remain faithful until the end (2:24-25). Both images depict life in the new age. The first promise is a free rendering of LXX Psalm 2:8-9 and *Psalms of Solomon* 17:23-24, a first-century BCE writing that interpreted Psalm 2 as a reference to the Messiah. LXX Psalm 2:8-9 reads, "You shall shepherd them with an iron rod; you shall shatter them like an earthen vessel" (author translation). *Psalms of Solomon* 17:24 reads, "To shatter all their material possessions with an iron rod, to destroy the lawless nations with the word of his mouth" (author translation). These passages from LXX Psalm 2, Psalms of Solomon 17, and Revelation share features. Each presents the Messiah as a righteous judge. Also, in each passage the rod serves as a symbol of judgment. However, in Revelation the iron rod is the spoken

16. See my complete argument in *Christ and Community*, 127–32; cf. Murphy, *Fallen Is Babylon*, 131–33.

17. Beale makes a similar point (*Revelation: Shorter*, 68–69).

word as evidenced in Revelation 19:15. These passages indicate a Second Temple Jewish messianic reading of Psalm 2. Revelation transforms this tradition to refer to a spoken witness constituting the means of ruling. Revelation 20:4-6 fulfills the promise to rule and to share authority. The morning star is Christ himself: "I'm . . . the bright morning star" (22:16), the fulfillment of the second promise. It conveyed a close, eternal, unbroken fellowship between God/Christ and the faithful (21:9–22:5). Fidelity, victory, and an unbroken fellowship have become synonymous terms.

Sardis

There is little condemnation in this message. Rather, the community is encouraged to do more because it is on the brink of death.

The fifth promise is found in Revelation 3:5. Christ chastises some for not fulfilling their potential as Christians (3:2-4). The victors will wear white, their names shall never be removed from the scroll of life and Christ "will declare their names" before God Almighty and his angels. White clothing symbolized purity and goodness. The color white occurs fifteen times in Revelation and has negative connotations only in 6:2 (e.g., 7:9-14; 19:11-14). It communicated to the original audience their religious and ethical propriety.[18] Thus their names shall never be removed from the registry of the citizens of the New Jerusalem. Christ shall call their names before God Almighty. The white clothing and the two mentions of the name constitute two sides of one soteriological sequence. The white clothing connoted the ethical purity of the faithful; the two names refer to the resulting reward that awaited the faithful. This promise is fulfilled in 20:11-15. At no point are Christians instructed to take up arms to defeat evil but by witnessing faithfully even unto death.

Philadelphia

The Christian community in Philadelphia receives praise from Christ for its fidelity in the face of social pressure to conform to more traditional views and practices.

18. Cf. Witherington, *Revelation*, 105–6; Murphy, *Fallen Is Babylon*, 147–49; Koester, *Revelation*, 314.

One finds a familiar sequence of promises in the message to Philadelphia. The promise actually begins in Revelation 3:10: "Because you kept my command to endure, I will keep you safe through the time of testing." One must note again that the substance of the victory is remaining faithful. The promise in 3:12 states that Christ will make the victors pillars in God's temple, that they shall never leave it, and Christ will write the name of God, God's city, and "my own new name" on them.

Becoming pillars in the temple meant that Christians would never leave the presence of God. They shall become unmovable. This conveyed that there would be an unbroken fellowship between God and God's people (see 21:1-8). Indeed, each person will be a priest who can approach God in the New Jerusalem. This would be the opposite of the exclusion Christians experienced from the synagogue. It also contrasts with Asian social exclusion and harassment.

The names are again one and the same name, and that name is probably *Christian*. This would have said to the original recipients of the Apocalypse that while *Christian* was a badge of shame in Asian society, in actuality it was the badge of honor in heaven. Writing this name upon each of them symbolized a sealing that protects the Philadelphians from eternal damnation (see Ezek 9:4). All this imagery conveyed grace, salvation, and loving benefaction.

Honor and Shame

Many Mediterranean societies in the first century CE operated to a large degree on the principle of honor and shame. People strove to perform acts of virtue that would bring honor to themselves and to their extended community. Conversely, people strove to avoid shameful acts that would bring shame to themselves and to those in their families, communities, and nations.

Laodicea

Christians in Laodicea have become "lukewarm." They either do the right things for the wrong reasons or they espouse proper beliefs but do not follow up with proper ethics. In any event, Christ describes them in very negative terms. They must come back to him and relearn what it means to be Christians (3:14-19).

In the message to Laodicea, the victors will sit with Christ on his throne (see fulfillment in 20:4) as Christ sits on a throne with God (3:14). In other words, God Almighty shares authority with Christ who in turn shares it with the faithful. "To the person who conquers in this fashion, who witnesses in spite of the risks, Christ will issue the same reward God gave Christ as a result of his testimony. He will give them a seat on his heavenly throne."[19]

This sharing sequence would assure Asian Christians of their ethical purity, good deportment, and ultimate vindication through their faithful witnessing. It would convey to them that the "word of God" and "the witness of Jesus" are one and the same and that if they have the same witness, they are one with God and Christ (see 6:9-11 and 20:4-6). It would also envision a glorious outcome, sharing God's throne. The victors became victorious by remaining faithful throughout their suffering.

In these seven messages, *nikao* and *nike* have been transformed from references to victory, conquering, and overcoming in athletic, political, or military terms, into references to emerging victorious by sustaining a faithful witness, even if that faithfulness leads to one's death (e.g., 2:13). Emerging victorious through suffering has become the Christian modus vivendi. It is this new transformation of power that becomes the mark of a Christian in the Book of Revelation and it is based upon the crucifixion and resurrection of Christ.

Nikao in Other Key Passages

So I looked, and there was a white horse. Its rider held a bow and was given a crown. And he went forth from victory [*nikon*] to victory [*nikese*].[20] (Rev 6:2)

Revelation 6:2 is the first of the seven seals and the much-discussed mini-cycle of the four horsemen of the Apocalypse. The rider on the first

19. Blount, *Revelation*, 84.

20. Another possible translation might be "And I looked, and behold, a white horse, and the one who sat upon it had a bow and a crown was given to him and he went out conquering so that he might also conquer." John's Greek is far from stellar.

horse has caused much discussion. Is the rider the same figure one finds in 19:11, or the Parthian leader Vologeses, or the anti-Christ, or another military/political figure of the Roman era? While the rider brings to mind many figures in antiquity, the rider is not the primary referent. The horse is the primary referent and that is why the horse is mentioned first. With the breaking of each seal, each horse brings about another eschatological woe that must be endured by all persons, saint and sinner alike. There is no rapture in John's Apocalypse. The rider is an angelic precursor of the Divine Warrior (DW) who rides a white horse in Revelation 19:11-21. In the same way, Michael is a precursor in Revelation 12:7 to Christ as the DW in Revelation 19:11. All three relate to the coming eschatological tribulations.

The rider has been given a crown and a bow. The crown (*stephanos*) connoted victory in competition (see 2:10; 3:11; 4:4, 10) and connects with Jesus's means of overcoming by suffering and being empowered to be enthroned with God Almighty in 3:21.[21] The white horse and the crown bring to mind images of a triumphant commander in a victory parade after he has conquered an opponent. The crown has been given by God, implying that God has either caused these things to occur or has allowed them.[22]

The Christian community must remain spiritually strong throughout the end-time trials. This fact has escaped many contemporary Christians for two reasons. First and foremost, most North American and European Christians do not live under duress and constant pressure to conform or change their beliefs. They assume the biblical context is no different. Second, many assume that they shall be raptured and escape these trials, as in the Gospels (e.g., Matt 24:36-44). John's Apocalypse understands that strong beliefs and faith are two very different things (e.g., 2:14-15; 3:1-3, 15-19). One may hold certain beliefs but acquiesce under pressure. True faith, however, informs one's actions and empowers one's life. Blount states it well: "Their faithfulness will matter as much as it does because they will perform it in the circumstance of such duress, just as Christ

21. Thomas and Macchia, *Revelation*, 155–56.

22. Murphy, *Fallen Is Babylon*, 205.

himself did on the cross."[23] Rowland writes, "To 'conquer,' therefore is to be like the Lamb, to do the Lamb's work and to be faithful like the Lamb. The reward will be to share the state that Jesus has (3:21),"[24] which is to sit enthroned with God and Christ (20:4). Victory comes through witnessing faithfully to the word of God and the witness of Christ Jesus, and not through power.

> When they [the two witnesses] have finished their witnessing, the beast that comes up from the abyss will make war on them, gain victory over [*nikesei*] them and kill them. (Rev 11:7)

This passage gives an example of the traditional use of *nikao* in Greek literature: the beast from the abyss physically conquers the two witnesses. However, their defeat is temporary and ultimately leads to their exaltation (11:11-12).

The two witnesses are symbolic figures. They resemble angels in part due to their nearness to God; and they also function as prophets due to their revelatory purpose. They also provide an example for earthly Christians to follow through their fervent witness. Symbolic references always have multiple meanings, particularly in apocalypses.[25] The two witnesses represent both these functions to some degree.

The two witnesses as olive trees in Revelation 11:4 probably derive from Zechariah 4, where they symbolize Joshua, the high priest, and Zerubbabel, the governor. The two lampstands in 11:4 symbolized the temple. "The message (in Zechariah 4)... was that God was in charge of rebuilding the temple, and his Spirit would overcome their opponents and guide the two leaders in the completion of the task."[26] In Revelation, they primarily represent a faithful Christian community under duress. The task of the witnesses and the church during this final period of world history is to keep the faith, even in the midst of tremendous social

23. Blount, *Revelation*, 123.

24. Rowland, *NIB* 12:611.

25. Cf. Murphy, *Fallen Is Babylon*, 262–68. See also L. L. Thompson, *The Book of Revelation: Apocalypse and Empire* (New York: Oxford University Press, 1990), 37–91.

26. Osborne, *Revelation*, 420–21, quote from 421; cf. Beale, *Revelation: Shorter*, 227.

pressure to change. Osborne argues, "And the task of witness is to maintain their 'conquering' perseverance and to witness even by their death (cf. 12:11)."[27]

The beast who comes from the abyss in 11:7 is an evil figure. It comes and conquers the two witnesses, who represent goodness and righteousness. The two witnesses have followed the example of Christ (e.g., 1:5; 3:14), Antipas (2:13), John himself (1:9), and the martyrs (6:9). The work of the two witnesses is not to bear arms but to bear witness. Their exaltation to heaven in 11:11-12 conveyed to the original recipients of the Apocalypse that their apparent defeat was actually their victory, a victory that has come through suffering. "Conquest by the beast cannot overcome that true 'conquest,' inspired by the Lamb" through the Lamb's faithful witness, death, and subsequent resurrection.[28] This would have said to Asian Christians under intense social pressure that their God would remember their fidelity and also rescue them from the second death (20:11-15).

This verse is another example of the traditional manner in which *nikao* functioned in Greco-Roman society:

> It (the beast from the sea) was also allowed to make war on the saints and to gain victory over [*nikesai*] them. (Rev 13:7)

Indeed, one could translate *nikao* "to conquer" since it is a Greek infinitive. John has a strong doctrine of omnipotence common among contemporary conservative Christians: God allows the beast to conquer the saints. John is reluctant to think that anything is beyond God's control. Moreover, this verse echoes Revelation 11:7, where the beast from the abyss made war with the saints and overcame them. It is noteworthy that Revelation 11:7 and 13:7 use *nikao* in the traditional ways, but both refer to evil activities against the saints.[29]

27. Osborne, *Revelation*, 424.

28. Rowland, *NIB* 12:642.

29. Cf. Blount, *Revelation*, 251–52; Thomas and Macchia, *Revelation*, 235.

> Then I saw what appeared to be a sea of glass mixed with fire. Those who gained the victory [*nikontas*] over the beast, its image, and the number of its name were standing by the glass sea, holding harps from God. (Rev 15:2)

The sea of glass is either a metaphor for God's throne (see 4:6), God's majesty,[30] or "a heavenly counterpart to the Red Sea."[31] It is probably all three to some degree. The expression "mixed with fire" connoted judgment.[32] Holding harps connoted victory over evil. Beale and Murphy observe that the sea was a place of chaos in ancient Israel. Often God Almighty overcame the chaos and brought order to the cosmos.[33] The victors conquered the beast because the Lamb had conquered first and "granted them a share in the effects of His victory at the sea. They are those who have refused to compromise their faith in the midst of pressure and persecution."[34] The scene conveyed to the original readers "something of the intensity of the faithful witnesses' conflict with the beast."[35] The victors stand on the other side of the sea, just as the Hebrews stood on the other side of the Sea of Reeds in Exodus 15. They stand before God's throne (cf. 6:9). They are beyond the chaos of the end times and its accompanying tribulations.[36]

Osborne writes, "The image of 'conquering' is one of the critical themes of the book and pictures the saints as victors over temptation, the pressures of the world, and the cosmic powers of evil. Even as the beast 'conquers' the saints by killing them, he is being 'conquered by' the saints and the Lamb."[37] Indeed, Christ, God's Son, who loved us and gave himself for us, laid the foundation on Golgotha. Asian Christians must now build the house with their own witnesses.

30. Osborne, *Revelation*, 562.

31. Beale, *Revelation: Shorter*, 317; cf. Murphy, *Fallen Is Babylon*, 329.

32. Cf. Thomas and Macchia, *Revelation*, 261–63; Beale, *Revelation: Shorter*, 317; Murphy, *Fallen Is Babylon*, 329.

33. Beale, *Revelation: Shorter*, 317–18; Murphy, *Fallen Is Babylon*, 329.

34. Beale, *Revelation: Shorter*, 317–18.

35. Thomas and Macchia, *Revelation*, 269.

36. Cf. Rowland, *NIB* 12:672–73.

37. Osborne, *Revelation*, 562–63.

To Be Crucified with Christ

I have been crucified with Christ and I no longer live, but Christ lives in me. And the life that I now live in my body, I live by faith, indeed, by the faithfulness of God's Son, who loved me and gave himself for me. (Gal 2:20)

Adopt the attitude that was in Christ Jesus:
Though he was in the form of God,
he did not consider being equal with God something to exploit.
But he emptied himself
by taking the form of a slave
and by become like human beings.
When he found himself in the form of a human,
he humbled himself by becoming obedient to the point of death,
even death on a cross. (Phil 2:5-8)

Unbroken Fellowship

> Those who emerge victorious [*nikon*] will inherit these things. I will be their God, and they will be my sons and daughters. (Rev 21:7)

What are "these things" that will be inherited? They are eternal fellowship with God Almighty (21:1-3). Specifically, God shall personally wipe away their tears, death will no longer be a threat, nor will mourning, sadness, or pain. All physical needs, such as hunger and thirst, will be gone. These afflictions will be history. That is the inheritance prepared for those who emerge victorious, those who will become the children of God and reside in the New Jerusalem (21:4-7; see also 2:11). Moreover, the victors/conquerors in 21:1-7 should be contrasted with those mentioned in 21:8 who have been unfaithful, immoral, or both.

Revelation 21:7 also echoes many biblical passages that promise an unbroken fellowship between God and God's people. Leviticus 26:12 reads, "I will walk among you; I will be your God and you will be my people." This passage from the Torah would have been the source for similar passages in the Hebrew Bible for John. This particular passage comes in a series of promises to Israel contingent upon Israel's faithfulness. The final promise in Leviticus 26 contains the indwelling of God among God's people. "This God set Israel free from bondage in Egypt (26:13) and enabled Israel to walk without despondency and without the yoke of the heavy burdens of making bricks."[38] John provides a vision of the ultimate fulfillment of this promise that liberates the New Israel not from Egypt but from the despondencies of the Roman world.[39] It is contingent upon the faithfulness of the New Israel described in Revelation 7.

In 2 Samuel 7:11-16, God promises to establish the Davidic dynasty and to never take his love from David, even if God must discipline him. In the midst of this promise God says, "I will be a father to him, and he will be a son to me" (7:14). In Jeremiah, the people Israel replace David with a similar promise: "And I thought, You will call me father, and you won't turn from me" (3:19). In the midst of a restoration passage, we find these words: "You will be my people, and I will be your God" (Jer 30:22). Revelation makes an additional transition and envisions a New Israel composed of persons from all nationalities and ethnicities (see 7:9; cf. Eph 2:11-22). Humans from every nationality, culture, and language shall have "a familial relationship with God."[40]

Those who have emerged victorious have previously suffered, but they have held fast to their beliefs and not wavered under social pressure. "They are the ones who have overcome the beast and its image by means of the blood of the Lamb."[41] Victory comes through suffering.

The pattern noted earlier in the chapter, where we found the transformation of *nikao* and *nike* to convey why victory comes through a faithful, steadfast witness, has recurred in our discussions of Revelation 6:2, 13:7, 15:2, and 21:7. In the instances where this is not the case (11:7 and 13:7), the Apocalypse depicts the evil vanquishing of the saints by a fiendish beast. Thus, the references to victory coming through the exercising of power are references to evil.

38. W. C. Kaiser Jr., "The Book of Leviticus," *NIB* 1:1179–80.

39. Cf. Murphy, *Fallen Is Babylon*, 406–15.

40. Osborne, *Revelation*, 721.

41. Osborne, *Revelation*, 721.

Our attention turns now to Christ as the Divine Warrior, where we see the same transformation of power in this image of Christ.

The Divine Warrior (Rev 19:11-21)

Christ appears as a Divine Warrior (DW) in Revelation 19:11-21. The image of the DW continues the christological message associated with the Human One/Son of Man and the slain Lamb. John's Apocalypse has a coherent christological presentation.[42] This section will discuss the passage and in the process identify ways in which the DW reinforces and complements the Human One/Son of Man and the slain Lamb images. Even as the DW, Christ does not conquer with arms but with a faithful spoken witness, and he stains his robe with his own blood.

The DW was empowered by God Almighty to judge and make war justly (19:11). Both the symbolic names given to the DW, a concept highly dependent upon Isaiah 63, as well as the imagery associated with the DW, indicate that the DW is God's eschatological divine agent who acts in God's stead.

The DW appears in 19:11 on a white horse and receives the name "Faithful and True." The white horse symbolizes purity and also brings to mind the image of a victorious conqueror returning home.[43] The name "Faithful and True" echoes 1:5 ("the faithful witness") and 3:14 ("the faithful and true witness"), which refer to the Human One/Son of Man. In Revelation 21:5 and 22:6, we read that God Almighty's words are "trustworthy and true." The Greek in 3:14, 19:11, 21:5, and 22:6 all read *pistos kai alethinos* and can be rendered into English either "faithful and true" or "trustworthy and true."[44] This phrase connects the Human One/Son of Man and the DW images with God Almighty. Throughout the book, God Almighty shares honors with Christ Jesus, for example, as evidenced by the hymns in Revelation 4–5.[45] In this instance, Christ's

42. I make this argument in more detail in *Christ and Community* (202–08, 236–45).

43. See my article on "White" in *Eerdman's Dictionary of the Bible*, ed. D. N. Freedman (Grand Rapids: Eerdman's Publishing, 2000), 1377.

44. See my "'*Pistos kai Alethinos*' in Revelation 19:11, 21:5 and 22:6," *Notes on Translation* 12 (1998): 31–33. Wycliffe translators rendered this article into French for French-speaking ministers in Africa. Modern translations should, at the very least, take note of this recurrence in their annotated editions.

45. Richard Bauckham has excellent discussions of this topic in *The Theology of the Book of Revelation* (New York: Cambridge University Press, 1993), 23–30, 54–65.

words are God's words, and Christ has the authority to speak for God Almighty. This would have been a powerful word of encouragement for suppressed Christians. It would have assured them of the righteousness of their religious conviction and the correctness of their religious practices.

In Revelation 19:12 the DW has "eyes...like a fiery flame," many royal crowns (*diademata*), and a name known only to him. The fiery eyes connect once again with the Human One/Son of Man in 1:14, whose eyes are described in the same way. This imagery connotes the right to judge. The royal crowns connoted regal status. The unknown name echoes 2:17, where the Spirit (that is the Human One/Son of Man) gives each Christian a new name known only to the one who receives it. Just as the world did not recognize its Savior in Christ, it will not recognize his followers either. This would have explained to Asian Christians at once why they were repressed and also how to endure it.

Revelation 19:13 has strong echoes of Isaiah 63. In Isaiah 63, the blood on the DW's robe is the blood of the enemies, but in Revelation 19:13 the blood is the DW's blood. In Revelation, Christ "emerges victorious" by shedding his blood (see 5:9, 12; 12:11). The use of traditional images in Revelation are often reinterpreted, giving old metaphors a freshness. The DW receives another name: "the Word of God." This new name communicated to Asian Christians that Christ Jesus is the full manifestation of the will of God in human history. What "Faithful and True" implies, "the Word of God" confirms. This name would have reasserted the message of assurance in the preceding verse.

The heavenly army accompanies the DW in 19:14. The army wears fine white and pure linen, and they ride on white horses. Again, the white horses and the white clothing convey purity. The army resembles the entourage that accompanies a returning victorious commander. This army is the same group encountered in 6:9-11, 7:3-8, and 14:5 and will be seen again in 20:4-6. They are the martyrs who have given their lives for the faith (cf. 12:10-11). Within Judaism, angels and the high priest on Yom Kippur wore linen and it denoted their purity and worthiness to approach God.[46]

46. E.g., Lev 16:4; Ezek 9:2-3; 10:1-8; Dan 12:3-7; 1 En. 62:15-16; Philo, *Mos.* 2.17.

In Revelation 3:4, the Human One/Son of Man states that the faithful will accompany him "clothed in white because they are worthy [*azios*]." *Azios* can mean "fitting," "deserving," or "appropriate." In 7:9, an international multitude of the saved stand before the throne of God dressed in white. The most significant passage is 19:8, where the bride of Christ receives "fine, pure white linen to wear, for the fine linen is the saints' acts of justice" (or "for the fine linen are the saints' righteous deeds"). The wedding imagery conveyed an intimate relationship between Christ and Christians (cf. Eph 5:21-33). Bright linen connoted righteousness. Revelation 15:6 describes angels "dressed in pure, bright linen" (author translation). Linen connoted purity and election. This imagery also conveyed to Asian Christians what was possible for them if they remained faithful. Righteousness comes not from being dressed appropriately but from acting appropriately. That is why the linen constitutes the righteous *deeds* of the saints. The martyrs are ready to end their eschatological exodus to the New Jerusalem.[47]

Revelation 19:15 describes how and why the DW will judge the enemies of God and God's people. The DW has a sharp sword protruding from his mouth that will defeat his adversaries. This recapitulates the vision of the Human One/Son of Man in 1:16. The DW will also rule with an iron rod, another image connected to the Human One/Son of Man (2:27). Finally, the DW will "trample the winepress" of God's wrath, reiterating God Almighty's action in 14:19. The sword from the DW's mouth is a metaphor for defeating one's enemies through a spoken witness: the witness is so effective that no other armament is necessary. Indeed, "These are the words of the Amen, the faithful witness" (3:14), or "They gained the victory over (*enikesan*) him [Satan] on account of the blood of the Lamb and the word of their witness" (12:11). Speaking truth to power has power.

47. One finds a common literary technique in John's apocalypse. As one moves through the prophecy, one finds more and more information revealed about a given image or concept. In this way, the book includes numerous interlocks that speak to the literary and theological unity of the work.

Speaking Truth to Power

Throughout the twentieth century, speaking truth to power transformed societies around the world: the Gandhi-led movement in India, the anti-apartheid movement in South Africa, the anti-Marcos movement in the Philippines, and the Solidarity movement in Poland all spoke truth to power and transformed their societies.

Ruling with an iron rod has an extensive tradition history. In Revelation 2:27, the Human One/Son of Man promises the victors they shall share authority with him and rule the nations with an iron rod. In Revelation 12:5, the newborn Messiah will rule with an iron rod. These passages probably have been influenced by Isaiah 11:4 and the LXX Psalm 2:9 traditions. Isaiah 11:4 says a Davidic Messiah "will strike the violent with the rod of his mouth," a judgment passage. LXX Psalm 2:9 states that the Messiah will lead with an iron rod. Psalms of Solomon 17:24 interprets both these passages from a messianic perspective by reading, "To shatter all their material possessions with an iron rod, to destroy the lawless nations with the word of his mouth" (author translation). All three present the Messiah as a righteous judge punishing evil nations. All employ the image of the rod as a means of judgment. The spoken word is a powerful means of overcoming evil. Revelation 19:15 has the same features. God, Christ, and the Christian community stand on one side; Satan and his minions stand on the other. Christians defeat Satan through their testimony.

Revelation 19:16 ends this first section of this vision. The name "King of kings and Lord of lords" repeats the same title for the Lamb in 17:14 and is the last of the four names. It completes the others. This title normally was reserved for God Almighty and denoted God Almighty's sovereignty (e.g., Deut 10:17; LXX Dan 4:37; 1 En. 9:4; 1 Tim 6:15). This title in Revelation conveyed to Asian Christians that Christ, whether depicted as the Lamb or the DW, is God's divine representative and has the authority to act in God's stead. Christ is "ruler of the kings of the earth" (1:5).

Lord of Lords, King of Kings

And they said to their Lord, the King, Lord of lords, God of gods, King of kings. (1 En. 9:4)[48]

I confess and praise (him) because he is God of gods and Lord of lords and King of kings. (LXX Dan 4:37, author translation)

The second section relates the defeat of God's adversaries and their cohort. In 19:1-18, an angel invites persons to a ghoulish meal, "God's great supper" of unrighteous persons great and small (cf. 8:13). Verses 19-20 give the narrative of the defeat of the beast, the false prophet, and their followers. The followers of the beast and false prophet were defeated by the sword from the DW's mouth. This is a metaphor for a powerful spoken witness, which destroys evil. In no instance does the army accompanying the DW actually engage in battle. "As made clear in 5:5-6, the true victory was won on the cross, and the final battle in 19:17-21 is only the last act of defiance by an already defeated foe."[49]

This chapter has examined the transformation of *nikao* and *nike* in the Book of Revelation from athletic victory or vanquishing militarily or politically to maintaining a faithful witness regardless of the eventual outcome. Victory is sustained through suffering. Power is redefined as conquest through nonviolent witness, a witness that sustains itself against institutional and social pressures to conform. It is an inner strength that sustains the inner person so that the outer person can remain true to personal beliefs and practices without yielding.

This suffering did not derive from any illegal or immoral activity but from merely being a faithful Christian witness through word and deed. Indeed, victory through suffering came as a response to regional repression of Christians by local officials as well as pressures from more traditional Jewish persons. Christians were under pressure to accommodate themselves to local religio-political customs. The issue of whether to eat meat offered to idols was one such case. While some saw no problems with

48. M. A. Knibb, trans., "1 Enoch," *AOT*.

49. Osborne, *Revelation*, 122.

eating meat offered to nonexistent idols, John saw it as an inappropriate accommodation to culture.

Furthermore, traditional Jewish persons would not have liked the fact that Christians gave divine honors to Jesus. For them, this would have been seen as a step toward polytheism, a compromise to pagan values. In turn, Asian Christians are not told to respond with force but with faithful steadfastness. It is God's role to judge, reprove, and to save (e.g., Revelation 18 and 20:7-15).

Finally, this transformation of *nikao/nike* is consistent with the image of the slain Lamb who conquers evil by dying for the faith and replacing the lion in Revelation 5.

Justice and Grace

"God has two outstretched arms. One is strong enough to surround us with justice, and one is gentle enough to embrace us with grace."

—*Martin Luther King Jr.*[50]

In the second part of the current chapter, we have seen the DW who conquers through the sword from his mouth, that is, through a strong verbal witness. In no way is violence overcome by either political or military means. The army that accompanies the DW never engages in battle, as is true with the army in the vision in Revelation 14:1-5. Evil is overcome by witnesses, not weapons. In these instances, faith is not merely a set of doctrines to which one adheres verbally, which one may abandon under pressure or when it becomes convenient. Faith is a way of life. It inhabits one's body, mind, and entire being. Faith is the power given by God to Christians to acknowledge but to overcome fears. It is the power to endure under extreme circumstances. Such faith is a power that only God can give.

50. Martin Luther King Jr., "A Tough Mind and a Tender Heart," *Strength to Love* (Minneapolis, MN: Fortress, 2010), 8.

Study Questions

1. How does the Apocalypse transform the concept of conquering?
2. How does the victory through suffering motif manifest itself outside the letters to the seven churches?
3. Where are the signs of the repression of Christians in the messages to the seven churches?
4. Is the concept of honor and shame still a social factor today? If so, how? If not, why?
5. What are the similarities and dissimilarities between the Divine Warrior in Isaiah 63:1-6 and Revelation 19:11-21?
6. What groups speak truth to power today?

Chapter 4

APPLYING THE APOCALYPSE

This study summarizes the arguments concerning the date and the social setting for John's Apocalypse (chapter 1), the presentation of the slain Lamb as the central christological concept of John's Apocalypse (chapter 2), and the transformation of the concept of power (chapter 3). This final chapter identifies ways in which both the academy and the parish have not fully understood the Apocalypse and how a more accurate perspective of the Apocalypse might benefit academic research and congregational life.

Chapter 1 examines the social setting of the Apocalypse. Relying on the internal evidence of the book itself, we learned that the book was probably written between 68 and 70 CE. Discussions such as who is or is not an apostle; a Jewish self-identity; the temple still standing; including Galba, Otho, and Vitellius among the emperors; and whether or not to eat meat offered to idols are all more intelligible in the late 60s than the early 90s.

Additionally, it appears that the book was written in a social setting where Christians were still a part of the Jewish community; in other words, the Apocalypse is a Christian Jewish book. In 2:9 and 3:9 John does not criticize some of his opponents because they are Jews. He criticizes them for not being righteous, faithful Jews. Being Jewish is still the religious ideal. John understands Christianity to be the truest form of Judaism. Christians would have had tensions with more theologically traditional Jewish persons due to the Christian belief that God Almighty shared divine honors with Jesus. More traditional Jewish persons would have perceived this as polytheism and possibly blasphemy. While some contemporary Christians may decry this response by some groups within Judaism, many contemporary Christians hold similar positions about other Christian movements, to say nothing of other religions altogether.[1]

Jewish Christianity had its own internal tensions, prior to the severe break that came at the end of the first century. John sees those persons who eat meat offered to idols, the Jezebel movement, the Balaam-Balak group, and the Nicolaitans as illegitimate pretenders to the true faith or, at best, the inappropriate chief rivals for adherents within the seven churches. For John, the central question seems to focus on who speaks for Jesus. While the apostles and the apostolic tradition are important, John never appeals to apostolic authority and he does not refer to the apostles as if he were one of them. John's authority comes directly from Jesus by means of prophetic visions. In this sense, John and Paul have something in common.

Finally, there are tensions with the social fabric of the imperial cult in the Roman province of Asia. Price and Friesen have demonstrated how the imperial cult was deeply embedded in Asian society and how it helped to make sense of the current world order within the larger polytheistic pantheon at both the personal level and the society as a whole. For Christians not to participate in the imperial cult would seem inexplicable and incomprehensible for Asian citizens.[2] These social conflicts would have placed Christians in a very precarious position within Asian society.

This overview of the social context also has the potential to inform our present-day social settings—academic and religious. A more accurate reading of the social context of the Apocalypse clarifies certain debates. For example, we hear another voice and another rationale in the debate about eating meat offered to idols.[3] Also, while the messages in Revelation

1. Many contemporary Christian denominations do not accept either the ordination or the baptism of other Christian denominations. Many individual congregations do not accept ordinations or baptisms done in other congregations.

2. We should think how angry some persons become when at sporting events someone does not stand for the national anthem or when someone does not bow during prayer.

3. It would be good to hear Peter's or Barnabas's perspectives on the incident in Antioch recorded in Galatians 2:11-21.

2–3 primarily addressed internal matters, when they do address the wider social context they comment upon Christian suffering (e.g., 2:13), a fact continuously overlooked by many contemporary New Testament scholars. A proper reading of the messages may lead to more insights about Roman society, in general, and the seven churches in Asia, in particular.

In chapters 2 and 3, we also noted three significant transformations: (1) the transformation of the chief messianic image from a lion to a slain lamb, (2) the transformation of the term *nikao* and its cognates from the use of power to passive resistance, and (3) the transformation of the term *martyrs* from witnessing in court to bearing a faithful witness for one's religious beliefs, even if it meant death. *These three transformations are inseparable in the Book of Revelation.* The first two transformations occurred concurrently in Revelation 5:5-6. When John turns to see the Lion who has conquered (*enikesen*), he sees instead a lamb who has been slain (*esphagmenon*). From this point on, *nikao* ceases being a military, political, or athletic term, but one connoting spiritual strength and the slain Lamb becomes the dominant messianic image in the Apocalypse. Moreover, the concept of the Lamb now informs how Christians are to defeat evil—as witnesses and not warriors.

The Lion of Judah was a major messianic image in Second Temple Judaism. It symbolized a hoped-for Messiah like David who would restore the spiritual and political fortunes of Israel (see 2 Esd 11–13; Matt 2–3; Luke 1:26-33). The crucifixion and the resurrection have transformed the expectation and turned it upon its head. The lion has been replaced by the Lamb of God. The Messiah has not completed a military campaign but has conquered the hearts and minds of men and women. On Good Friday it was evident that Jesus was the victim, but that defeat was merely a battle and not the end of a war. On Easter morning, the victim became the victor: victory came through witnessing faithfully, suffering for the faith, and only then came ultimate vindication. The One who was deemed discourteous and disobedient in the Roman court of law has been deemed civilized and obedient in the heavenly court.

The third transformation initially appears in Revelation 1:2 and 1:5, where John bears witness to the "word of God and to the witness of Jesus

Christ," connecting God's word, Jesus's witness, and John's Apocalypse, and where Jesus Christ is "the faithful witness, the firstborn from among the dead." This connects Jesus's faithfulness to Jesus's death, a motif that will recur throughout the Apocalypse. Christians must remain faithful to Christ (as Christ was faithful to God) even if it means giving one's life for one's faith. Just as Christ Jesus was faithful to his Father and died on the cross, his followers must be faithful to him. Moreover, just as Christ Jesus "emerged victorious" on Easter morning, so too will his followers who remain faithful, regardless of the consequences, "emerge victorious" at the Judgment.

Jesus, the Davidic Messiah

When Elizabeth was six months pregnant, God sent the angel Gabriel to Nazareth . . . to a virgin who was engaged to a man named Joseph, a descendent of David's house. The virgin's name was Mary. (Luke 1:26-27)

This would have been a powerful message to Asian Christians in a Roman context feeling pressure to conform to both Jewish and pagan religious expectations, as well as feeling tensions with other Christian groups who were probably more accommodating to their social context. This message provided two explanations simultaneously. First, it explained to Christians why they were suffering. Christ had suffered and so will they. It also said to them that Christ identified with their plight,[4] making their pain understandable in the broader cosmic and soteriological context. Second, it explained how they could overcome their situation by sustaining a faithful witness, even if it meant their death. They are witnesses, not warriors. The Resurrection said that God remembers the faithful and ultimately turns the victims into victors (Rev 20:11–21:8).

Accompanying the metamorphosis of messianic images and messianic expectations is the change rendered to *nikao* and *nike*. They are changed from political, military, and athletic terms for overpowering or defeating

4. Howard Thurman makes the same argument in *Jesus and the Disinherited* (Boston: Beacon, 1996) in comparing the plight of African Americans in the twentieth century and the plight of Jews in the first century. See also Obery M. Hendricks Jr., *The Politics of Jesus* (New York: Three Leaves, 2006).

one's opponent into religious terms. They become the means to overcome evil in the world, not through arms or force but through witnessing for one's faith (*marturia*; e.g., 12:11; 20:4-6). Christ emerged victorious through his death (5:5-9). He is not the lion but the slain Lamb who conquers through his faithful witness (1:5). Christians are not encouraged to take up arms but to willingly confess their faith and to trust God for the victory (6:9-11). When this occurred before Roman provincial officials or before local authorities who participated in the imperial cult, it is civil disobedience: a respectful, well-mannered response to what Christians considered an unjust requirement.

Throughout the Apocalypse, the Lamb conquers through his faithfulness, not military or political power. Each of the promises to the victors in Revelation 2–3 demand a strong, faithful witness in the face of adversity. Military language is indeed employed, but it is always used to convey the difficulty of surviving the coming end-time trials with one's faith intact. Military imagery is integral to apocalyptic language (e.g., 1 En. 90:9-16) as well as early Christian discourse (e.g., Eph 6:10-20). In neither instance do we expect the audience of 1 Enoch or Ephesians to actually take up arms. Christians are admonished to affirm their faith in public, but they are never told to take up arms, nor do we see Christians taking up arms in the Apocalypse. Even when an army of Christians accompanies Christ (14:1-5 and 19:11-21), they never engage in the battle. It is always God Almighty (see 6:10), or Christ in God's stead, who defeats the enemy (19:21). There is indeed violence in the Apocalypse, but it is God's doing and not the church's doing. Judgment belongs to God; witnessing belongs to Christians.

Revelation 12:11 provides the key passage for understanding how the Apocalypse uses *nikao* and *martyria*. The battle is in heaven, and it is between Michael and his angelic army and Satan and his angelic army. Michael's army defeats (*enikesan*) Satan's army through "the blood of the Lamb and the word of their witness [*martyrias*]. Love for their own lives didn't make them afraid to die." This is very different from Michael's roles in Daniel 10:13-21, 12:1, and the Qumran *War Scroll* where Michael engages in battle.[5] In the Apocalypse, Michael does not actually engage in battle, because the Lamb's blood, as well as "their witness" (presumably the witness of Michael and his angels), have already defeated Satan. The remainder of the verse implies that Michael and his angels defeated Satan by dying: "Love for their own lives didn't make them afraid to die."[6] Again we note that *nikao* does not connote armed engagement, but witnessing faithfully, that is, standing firm in one's faith in the face of death. In the first-century Mediterranean world, there was a widespread belief that what occurs in the heavens will be repeated on Earth. This would have said to Asian Christians that a stalwart witness defeats Satan in heaven as well as on Earth.

The study also examined five key passages where *nikao* was the principle verb (6:2; 11:7; 13:7; 15:2; 21:7). It was noted that *nikao* depicts evil actions in 11:7 and 13:7 where the beast kills Christians, an example of the abuse of power. One might argue that 6:2 constitutes an evil act, but that is not the case. It is tragic, but it is not evil. Opening the first seal begins the sequence of end-time events which God Almighty has preordained. They are part and parcel of God's divine plan. Revelation 15:2 relates the story of those who were conquered by the beast, but stand victoriously on the safe side of the heavenly sea of glass. Revelation 21:7 tells the story of how the martyrs ultimately will reside in the New Jerusalem, with all its spiritual and physical benefactions, and will have eternal fellowship with God Almighty and Christ Jesus. They have conquered through their faithful witness, not through armaments.

This pattern was continued in the Divine Warrior passage (Rev 19:11-21). Traditionally, the Divine Warrior image depicted God as a cosmic military figure so powerful that he acts alone in defeating evil and bringing order to the cosmos. God uses physical power to overcome foes and to establish order. These motifs have deep roots in the ancient cultures of the eastern Mediterranean.[7] Here too the Divine Warrior-Christ does not engage in armed conflict but defeats his enemies with the sword that

5. Michael may be the angelic figure in 2 Macc 11:8 who appears in full armor and dressed in white.

6. The NASB reads, "and they did not love their life even when faced with death."

7. Cf. Adela Collins, *The Combat Myth in the Book of Revelation*, HDR 9 (Missoula, MT: Scholars, 1975).

comes from his mouth, a metaphor for a powerful spoken witness. It is the same witness that put John on Patmos (1:9) and led to Antipas's death (2:13), the death of the martyrs (6:9), and the death of Jesus (5:6). It is also the same witness that leads to Satan's expulsion from heaven (12:11), the blessedness for the saints (14:13), reigning with Christ (20:4-6), and entry into the New Jerusalem (21:1-7, 22:1-5). These passages would have encouraged Asian Christians to look beyond their problems to God's promises awaiting them in the New Jerusalem.

Scholarly Issues

The following four overarching issues recur in the academic study of John's Apocalypse: (1) the importance of getting the date correct; (2) the problem of narrow exegesis; (3) the perception of John as a "lone wolf" among New Testament writers; and (4) the response to fundamentalist Christian interpretations.

Most New Testament scholars believe that the date of the writing of the Apocalypse does not matter in the long run. The book either responds to a real regional crisis or it is the visionary fabrication of a lone Christian prophet. Earlier I noted that there are no allusions to the destruction of the second Jerusalem temple. Rather, the temple is still standing in Revelation 11:1. An earlier date for the book leads us to ask if John's Apocalypse might provide another perspective about the debate concerning the eating of meat offered to idols. If John's context was more hostile than Paul's, we wonder how widespread this debate might have been. It also correlates with other New Testament writings, such as Philippians and 1 Peter, which speak of Christians who suffered simply because of their faith. It also leads some to ask how influential apocalypticism was in early Christianity.[8] Scholars who work extensively in apocalyptic literature are aware of its influence in the New Testament, but those who do not are more likely to be aware of the findings of New Testament cultural anthropologists. Finally, an earlier dating explains why the book is so Jewish and so christocentric at the same time.

8. Greg Carey has recently published *Apocalyptic Literature in the New Testament* (Nashville: Abingdon Press, 2016), which examines the role of apocalypticism in early Christianity.

Perhaps the most significant issue concerning the dating of the Apocalypse is more theological and social than exegetical. Many biblical exegetes are probably reluctant to argue for an earlier date because they do not want to open the door into authoritarian disputes about apostolic authorship. It's true that many who argue for an earlier date do so to indirectly argue for apostolic authorship. However, the two questions are not mutually dependent.[9] Bell, Wilson, Rowland, and I put forth arguments for an earlier date without affirming apostolic authorship.[10]

Narrow exegesis is another liability when studying Revelation. Narrow exegesis occurs when one takes a single aspect of the book (that is genuinely there), turns it into a single-issue agenda, and interprets the entire book on the basis of that one perspective. While it might shine light on the book, it often does so in a vacuum as if that is all there is to learn about a given book.[11]

For example, for approximately two decades, New Testament scholars argued that Revelation did not display any degree of Christian suffering. Sweet argued that since the letters did not discuss Christian suffering but Christian laxity, then Christians were not under duress when John wrote.[12] Thompson argued that since there is no proof of an empire-wide

9. See my article "Dating the Apocalypse to John," *Bib* 84 (2003): 252–58.

10. I explicitly argue for an earlier date and against apostolic authorship. The two are not mutually inclusive ("Dating the Apocalypse to John, Revisited," *RevExp* 114 [2017]: 247–53).

11. Theological education is set up for this kind of imbalance when graduate students are required to write an original dissertation or when the academy forces specialization within a given field of study. Academic departments and schools force us to publish quickly in order to become tenured faculty so we publish on what we know. And groups and seminars at professional meetings repeatedly ask us to give our particular perspectives on panels and forums. Thus, vast areas of our subject go uncharted in order to be focused.

12. See J. P. M. Sweet, *Revelation* (London: SCM, 1979). Neither Sweet nor Thompson (see next note) believes there was a crisis at all. As a result they have ignored questions that might lead to another conclusion. For example, Sweet incorrectly assumed (without testing his thesis) that the seven letters were prose versions of the apocalyptic visions. Sweet is correct that there is a relationship between the seven messages and the apocalyptic visions, but not in the way he envisioned. Rather, the messages address internal matters while the apocalyptic visions depict external pressures on those communities. Both the letters and the visions address what the end will be for saints and sinners. Thompson correctly notes how the picture of Domitian has been distorted in order to present a negative and inaccurate view of him; however, he assumes (without proving) that no empire-wide persecution also means no regional suppression. The two are not mutually exclusive. Many New Testament scholars who agree with Sweet and Thompson also accept that 1 Peter, written to Christians in the same general area of the Roman Empire, does indeed address the repression of Christians.

persecution of Christians under Domitian, then Christians did not suffer in any way. Thompson implies that John projected a crisis that was never there.[13] This could not have occurred without narrow exegesis.

Along with narrow exegesis, there is the perspective that John was a lone wolf among New Testament writers. Admittedly, John alone penned an apocalypse in the New Testament canon, but John shares much with other New Testament writers. A few examples: John's Apocalypse is the only known apocalypse with epistolary features. It is probably no coincidence that John and Paul, who wrote many epistles, both had ministries in Roman Asia. Furthermore, both the Gospel of John and John's Apocalypse state that God Almighty and Christ Jesus share divine honors (compare John 1:1-14 and Rev 4–5). Also, 2 Corinthians 4:10-12, Colossians 1:24-29, and Philippians 1:27–2:11 view Christ's suffering as an explanation for Christian suffering and also witnessing faithfully as a means of overcoming it. Additionally, Revelation is not the only New Testament writing that sees Roman society as a hostile environment for Christians (e.g., Matt 10:16-23; John 15:21; Acts 5:41; 1 Pet 4:14). Finally, many New Testament writings use military imagery to describe how difficult it would be to maintain a Christian lifestyle in first-century Roman society (e.g., 1 Cor 15:24-26; 2 Cor 6:7; 1 Thess 5:8; 2 Thess 2:8; Eph 6:10-20).[14] John was not alone in some of his theological positions and his perspective of how the greater society viewed Christians negatively. Influenced heavily by the prophetic tradition and also early Jewish apocalypticism, John gave his analysis of the world through an apocalypse.

Biblical scholars, especially in the introductory classroom, wrestle with the problem of how to respond to Christian fundamentalist interpretations of the Revelation to John. Many fundamentalists engage in endless end-time speculation, and they preach a grace-free fire-and-brimstone message. The Left Behind series is the most developed and lucrative form of this way of misinterpreting Revelation.

13. E.g., L. L. Thompson, *The Book of Revelation: Apocalypse and Empire* (Nashville: Abingdon Press, 1990).

14. Christopher Rowland discusses the difficulty of the last days in both Paul and Revelation ("Revelation," *NICB* 12:703–4); Craig R. Koester, *Revelation: A New Translation with Introduction and Commentary*, AB (New Haven, CT: Yale University Press, 2014), 753–54.

Many Christian fundamentalists and Pentecostals use the Book of Revelation as a guide to ascertain when Christ will return, always seeing it happening within their own lifetime. When it does not happen, cognitive dissonance goes on overdrive, and they merely recalibrate. This is done in spite of Christ's teaching that such knowledge is God's alone to possess. Matthew 24:36 reads, "But nobody knows when that day or hour will come, not the heavenly angels and not the Son. Only the Father knows." Jesus says in Acts 1:7, "It isn't for you to know the times or seasons that the Father has set by his own authority."[15] Such speculation clearly has no scriptural support, and when these (inappropriate) predictions do not come true, they merely make all Christians look silly. Such speculation is both wasteful and unfaithful. It is a waste of time and it attempts to replace living by faith with living by knowledge in order to manipulate. Paul teaches us that the Lord will come like a thief in the night. It is not ours to guess when it will occur, but to live lives worthy of the name Christian (1 Thess 5:1-11).

Free Grace versus Grace-Free

"Free grace" refers to the theological teaching that one cannot earn or purchase God's grace. God gives it freely. "Grace-free" refers to sermons that make little if any reference to free grace. Instead, these sermons and books try to scare people with the emphasis on making a public profession of faith or else going to hell. Such preaching develops few long-term Christians.

For example, the Left Behind series is a published set of fictionalized books that depict Christians as armed warriors fighting the forces of evil. A careful reading of the Apocalypse shows that the Left Behind series is entirely incorrect. Revelation tells Christians to be witnesses, not warriors. Christians defeat evil through their steadfast witness and trust God for the ultimate vindication. In other words, Christians are to put their faith in God, not in their guns.

15. Am I the only person who sees the inconsistency in being a fundamentalist who speculates on the date of the end of the world, on the one hand, and who affirms a literal interpretation and adherence to Scripture, on the other hand, when Scripture teaches one to not do what one is doing in the first place?

There is much in the Apocalypse that the Christian community in the West needs to hear. For example, what does it mean for a Christian to be in power? Is force justified then? Absolutely not! It means that we Christians should strive not to become beasts of the land and beasts of the sea toward our fellow humans. It means that we should see privilege as a responsibility and not a right. It means that judgment belongs to God alone because sometimes DNA evidence sets prisoners free. It means remaining humble because good intentions can lead to bad mistakes.[16]

Many Christian fundamentalists use Revelation to "convict" people of their sinful state, so that they might repent before Christ comes back. The Book of Revelation does not support this: "Let those who do wrong keep doing what is wrong. Let the filthy still be filthy. Let those who are righteous keep doing what is right. Let those who are holy still be holy" (Rev 22:11). Often those on the theological left say that there is no concept of grace in the book, but there is (e.g., Rev 1:4-6). The Book of Revelation concentrates more on judgment, which can be good or bad depending upon the evidence, than grace because its original recipients needed a word of hope to encourage them. Another word for hope is judgment. For the saints, judgment means eternal bliss and fellowship with God and the Lamb, but for others it means eternal torment and separation from God and the Lamb. Often it is difficult for persons who have not been hopeless to understand how precious hope (and judgment, that is, *justice*) can be for those without hope.

On the other hand, those on the political right have exploited judgment in Revelation to the exclusion of hope.[17] They have not recognized a community in peril that needed "a word from the Lord" in order to continue. For those in the Christian communities of Roman Asia, the Book of Revelation was a word of hope and inspiration from a loving God who sent his Son to die for us. It is an exhortation to a community under duress to follow Christ's example, so that they might emerge victorious at the Judgment. To and for those Christians, John's Apocalypse was good news!

16. On the day I wrote this chapter, NPR reported on Jerry Miller, a man who was convicted of committing a felony and spent twenty-six years in prison. He was ultimately exonerated by DNA evidence.

17. Some people might say that it is "on steroids."

This good news in John's Apocalypse has gone unnoticed by many in the West. So few of us are in situations that need assurance that our very lives have not been in vain. The myth of objectivity has had a long shelf life in biblical studies, but the truth is that none of us is thoroughly objective. We all see life from our own individual social locations. While that is limiting, there is benefit in working with others who have different social locations that might be more similar to the apocalyptic experience of the early Jewish Christians.

Church Issues

We have discussed fruitless, end-time speculation and an emphasis upon God's judgment as opposed to God's grace in Christian fundamentalism. John's Apocalypse poses three additional problems in the church: (1) fear of the unknown, (2) the abuse of military imagery in Revelation for political ends, and (3) whether Western Christianity is under duress.

For many Christians, Revelation is a scary book. Thus, they avoid it. This is true of pastors and laypersons. Many pastors avoid Revelation because it is not as straightforward as the rest of the New Testament. It is loaded with symbolic references and coded messages, the narrative repeats itself, the images are often very old and seem foreign to contemporary Christians, and many scholars debate what certain things mean. The Revelation to John has the same problems we find throughout the New Testament, but within the symbolic universe of apocalyptic thinking they are more frequent and more mystifying. Coupled with the fact that this book depicts the end of time, interpreting Revelation is a mountain too high for some to climb.

Such an attitude is understandable. Interpreting this book requires humility. However, there are passages that need to be heard by all Christians. When I was a pastor in Little Rock, Arkansas, at Connor Chapel AME Church, I preached a series of sermons on the Apocalypse. The sermons were developed as a teaching moment. The series came about because we visited a neighboring church and heard a sermon on the Apocalypse. The sermon was so bad that I knew it would take a series to undo it.

Connor was an inner-city parish. The socioeconomic levels were lower to upper middle class. Varying educational levels reflected the social strata. The congregation was theologically moderate in most ways. I preached messages of hope for six weeks. The response was overwhelmingly positive. I did not try to expound upon texts where I had little expertise or that I felt were not relevant for my congregation. I preached what I knew and only preached one sermon from Revelation 2–3. We can preach from this book without scaring people. We simply need to spend more time with it.[18]

A second problem is the misappropriation of the military imagery and the usurping of roles that John's Apocalypse gives solely to God. Since the first Gulf War, I get at least one telephone call from a news agency whenever fighting breaks out in the Middle East. They always ask the same question: Is the current conflict a sign of the end of time? Those on the theological right have erroneously joined interpretation of the Book of Revelation with Middle East politics. In practice their evangelical identity and theology have been hijacked by their thirst for power in political government. This is unfortunate, in part, because the Book of Revelation addresses matters in a totally different region: modern Turkey. Revelation says nothing about the Middle East. It has to be read into the text. Many on the right seek a biblical justification to go to war for political reasons, completely missing the fact that Revelation instructs us to witness, not go to war. God alone will destroy God's enemies in God's own time. While it may be appropriate to express bearing a faithful witness in military terms in some instances, one should not confuse the medium with the message. The message in Revelation is that Christians should only bear witness, not take up arms, and Christians must wait for God's judgment (see Rev 6:9-11; 21:5-7). This type of waiting takes faith that many do not have. Faithfulness does not always receive quick results.

Conversely, many from the theological and political left have decried the violence in the Apocalypse without noting that Christians are

18. Rowland's commentary on Revelation in the *New Interpreters' Bible* is an excellent resource for pastors preparing for sermons and Bible studies. Pablo Richard's *Apocalypse: A People's Commentary on the Book of Revelation* (Maryknoll: Orbis, 1995) is another.

admonished to bear witness strongly and they never engage in battle. The appropriate question to ask is this: How are we to understand the relationship between God's judgment and human witnessing? The answer: Christians must do their part to defeat evil by witnessing faithfully and trust God to keep God's promises to those who are faithful and wait for vindication. Again, this takes a great deal of faith.

A Case for Witnessing

Sometimes war is a necessary evil, but it is still an evil. It changes the people who, though innocent, must endure it in their country. It changes the course of history. It changes the warrior. What seems good at the time is not always good in the long run.

How would Iraq be different today if, instead of starting Gulf War II, the United States built more hospitals and schools in the northern and southern no-fly zones under US control? A much weakened Saddam Hussein would still be in power, but there would not have been a power vacuum for ISIS to fill after his death.

Finally, Western Christianity is not under duress. There is no "evil empire" in the West putting Christians in jail because they confessed their faith in Jesus. Jesus is not illegal in the West. This puts Americans and Europeans in a totally different social location than first-century Asian Christians. For example, many contemporary Americans believe strongly in Manifest Destiny, that the United States has been endowed by God to be the leader of this planet. Many American preachers proclaim a "prosperity gospel," which affirms that Christians are meant to receive material possessions and the good life. These ideas are far from the message in Revelation. Indeed, the original recipients of Revelation would have found the first message dangerous; the second, absurd.

One brief example will demonstrate the danger of beliefs like Manifest Destiny. During Soviet rule, the Russian Orthodox Church went underground. The church was so secretive that at times it was not clear who actually led Russian Orthodoxy. They did this so that the Soviet state would not imprison the leader. With the fall of the Soviet Union, Russian Orthodoxy came out of the closet. American missionaries went to Russia thinking they would convert many new Christians to Christ. What they found instead was a church that not only survived but thrived under Soviet suppression. An intergenerational Russian Orthodoxy was alive, well, and ready to go public.

Three decades later, the Russian Orthodox Church is a tool of the Russian state and is also an ardent supporter of Vladimir Putin. It endorses whatever the Russian government does. The state's program is the church's prayer. This is the danger of the church aligning itself too closely with the state. An imperfect human institution cannot speak for God. It can only hope to approximate the truth that God wants for all of us.

The "prosperity gospel" is just as dangerous. It substitutes one kind of good news (employment, material possessions, a meaningful relationship, etc.) for the Christian kind of good news.[19] It says to good people without material wealth and a comfortable life that their lives are not good enough. Their faith is not strong enough. Such preaching insults the true gospel of the slain Lamb and the martyrdoms of Peter, Paul, James, Justin Martyr, and so many other early Christians. It is false news and should not be tolerated. The church universal is at its best when it remembers the political prisoner, the widow, the orphan, and the immigrant (e.g., Exod 22:21-24; Ezek 18:16-17; Matt 25:31-36). The church universal is at its best when it is not building cathedrals but rebuilding lives.

The church universal is at its best when it is the conscience of the state, when it reminds the state that it has a responsibility to people and not to programs that become institutions in themselves, unencumbered by human need. Nowhere in Scripture does this message come through more clearly than in John's Apocalypse.

The church universal is at its best when it listens to what the Spirit has to say. Only then can she emerge victorious by witnessing, not making war.

19. I am amused by license plates on expensive cars that convey how God enabled the owner to purchase the vehicle, as if there are no Christians using public transportation or as if all rich people are saints or as if there are no lower-middle-class single Christians who feel blessed and happy. God is not a genie.

Study Questions

1. How might the Middle East be different today if there had been no second Gulf War?
2. What other issues in the church have hindered our understanding of John's Apocalypse?
3. Can you think of examples or personal stories where the misuse of the Apocalypse has soured the book for many other Christians?
4. Is your congregation "grace-free" or "free grace"?
5. Is there really a "separation of church and state" (First Amendment to the US Constitution) in the United States?

BIBLIOGRAPHY

Aland, Kurt, and B. Aland. *The Text of the New Testament*. Grand Rapids: Eerdmans, 1987.

Aune, David E. "The Form and Function of the Proclamation to the Seven Churches (Revelation 2–3)." *NTS* 36 (1990): 182.

———. *Revelation*. WBC 52A–C. Nashville: Thomas Nelson, 1997, 1998.

Balch, David. *Let Wives Be Submissive. SBLDS* 26. Chico, CA: Scholars Press, 1981.

Bauckham, Richard J. *The Climax of Prophecy: Studies in the Book of Revelation*. Edinburgh: Clark, 1993.

———. *The Theology of the Book of Revelation*. New York: Cambridge University Press, 1993.

Bauer, W., W. F. Arndt, and F. W. Gingrich. *A Greek-English Lexicon of the New Testament and Other Early Christian Literature*. Revised by F. W. Gingrich and F. W. Danker from W. Bauer's 5th ed. Chicago: University of Chicago Press, 1979.

Beale, G. K. *John's Use of the Old Testament in Revelation*. JSNTSup 166. Sheffield: Sheffield Academic Press, 1998.

———. *Revelation: A Shorter Commentary*. Grand Rapids: Eerdmans, 2015.

Bell, A. A., Jr. "The Date of John's Apocalypse: The Evidence of Some Roman Historians." *NTS* 25:93–102.

Blount, Brian K. *Revelation: A Commentary*. NTL. Louisville: Westminster John Knox, 2009.

Boring, M. Eugene. *I & II Thessalonians: A Commentary*. NTL. Louisville: Westminster John Knox, 2015.

———. *Revelation. Interpretation*. Louisville: Westminster John Knox, 1989.

Caird, George B. *A Commentary on the Revelation of St. John the Divine*. HNTC. New York: Harper & Row, 1966.

Carey, Greg. *Apocalyptic Literature in the New Testament*. Nashville: Abingdon Press, 2016.

Charles, Robert Henry. *A Critical and Exegetical Commentary on the Revelation of St. John*, 2 vols. New York: Scribner's Sons, 1920.

Charlesworth, James H., ed. *Old Testament Pseudepigrapha*, 2 vols. Garden City, NJ: Doubleday, 1983 and 1985.

Collins, Adela Yarbro. *The Combat Myth in the Book of Revelation*. HDR 9. Missoula, MT: Scholars Press, 1975.

———. *Crisis and Catharsis: The Power of the Apocalypse*. Philadelphia: Westminster, 1984.

Collins, John J., ed. *Apocalypse: The Morphology of a Genre*. Semeia 14. Missoula, MT: Scholars Press, 1979.

Elliott, John H. *A Home for the Homeless*. Philadelphia: Fortress, 1981.

Ellul, J. *Apocalypse*. New York: Seabury, 1977.

Ferguson, J. *The Religions of the Roman Empire*. Surrey, UK: Thames & Hudson, 1970.

Friesen, S. J. *Imperial Cults and the Apocalypse to John*. Oxford: Oxford University Press, 2001.

Green, J. B. *1 Peter*. THNTC. Grand Rapids: Eerdmans, 2007.

Heller, A. "Toward a Sociology of Knowledge of Everyday Life." *Cultural Hermeneutics*, 3:7–18.

Hendricks, Obery M., Jr. *The Politics of Jesus*. New York: Three Leaves Press, 2006.

Keck, Leander, gen. ed. *The New Interpreter's Bible*, 12 vols. Nashville: Abingdon Press, 1998.

Keener, Craig S. *Acts: An Exegetical Commentary*, 4 vols. Grand Rapids: Baker Academic, 2013.

King, Martin Luther, Jr. *Strength to Love*. Minneapolis: Fortress, 2010.

Koester, Craig R. *Revelation: A New Translation with Introduction and Commentary*. New Haven, CT: Yale University Press, 2014.

Kokkinos, N. *Antonia Augusta: Portrait of a Great Lady*. London: Routledge, 1992.

Kraybill, J. N. *Imperial Cult and Commerce in John's Apocalypse*. JSNTSup 132. Sheffield: Sheffield Academic Press, 1996.

Krodel, G. A. *Revelation*. ACNT. Minneapolis: Fortress, 1989.

Laws, Sophie. *In Light of the Lamb*. GNS 31. Wilmington, DE: Glazier, 1988.

Lohmeyer, E. *Die Offenbarung des Johannes*, 2nd ed. HNT 16. Tübingen: Mohr, 1953.

Murphy, F. J. *Fallen Is Babylon: The Revelation to John*. NTC. Harrisburg, PA: Trinity Press, 1998.

Osborne, Grant R. *Revelation*. BECNT. Grand Rapids: Baker Academic, 2002.

Pattemore, Stephen. *The People of God in the Apocalypse*. SNTSMS 126. Cambridge: Cambridge University Press, 2004.

Price, Simon. *Rituals and Power: The Roman Imperial Cult in Asia Minor*. Cambridge: Cambridge University Press, 1984.

Rowland, Christopher C. *The Open Heaven*. New York: Crossroads, 1982.

———. "Revelation" in *The New Interpreter's Bible*, 12:501–743. Nashville: Abingdon Press, 1998.

Scobie, C. H. H. "Local References in the Letters to the Seven Churches." *NTS* 39:606–24.

Sherwin-White, A. N. *The Letters of Pliny: A Historical and Social Commentary*. Oxford: Clarendon, 1966.

Slater, T. B. *Christ and Community: A Socio-Historical Study of the Christology of Revelation*. JSNTSup 178. Sheffield: Sheffield Academic Press, 1999.

———. "Context, Christology and Civil Disobedience in John's Apocalypse." *RevExp* 106:51–56.

———. "Dating the Apocalypse to John, Revisited." *RevExp* 114:247–53.

———. "On the Social Setting of the Revelation to John." *NTS* 44:232–56.

———. "*Pistos kai Alethinos* in Revelation 19:11, 21:5 and 22:6." *Notes on Translation* 12:31–33.

———. *The Son of Man in Second Temple Judaism*. Lewiston, NY: Mellen Press, 2017.

Smith, Mitzi K. and Yung Suk Kim. *Toward Decentering the New Testament: A Reintroduction*. Eugene, OR: Cascade Books, 2018.

Smith, Shanell. *The Woman Babylon and the Marks of Empire: Reading Revelation with a Postcolonial Womanist Hermeneutic of Ambiveilance*. Minneapolis: Fortress, 2014.

Sparks, H. F. D., ed. *The Apocryphal Old Testament*. Oxford, UK: Clarendon, 1984.

Stark, R. "The Class Basis of Early Christianity from a Sociological Model." *Sociological Analysis* 47:216–25.

Sumney, Jerry L. *Colossians*. NTL. Louisville: Westminster John Knox, 2008.

Sweet, J. P. M. *Revelation*. SCMPC. London: SCM, 1979.

Talbert, Charles H. *What Is a Gospel?* Philadelphia: Fortress, 1977.

Thomas, J. C., and F. D. Macchia. *Revelation*. THNTC. Grand Rapids: Eerdmans, 2016.

Thompson, Leonard. *The Book of Revelation: Apocalypse and Empire*. Oxford: Oxford University Press, 1990.

Thurman, Howard. *Jesus and the Disinherited*. Boston: Beacon, 1996.

Ulrichsen, J. H. "Die sieben Haupter und die zehn Horner: Zur Datierung der Offenbarung des Johannes." *ST* 39:1–20.

Walbank, F. W. *The Hellenistic World*. Cambridge, MA: Harvard University Press, 1982.

Wall, Robert W. *Revelation*. NIBC. Peabody, MA: Hendrickson, 1991.

Wilson, J. C. "The Problem of the Domitianic Date." *NTS* 39:597–605.

Witherington, Ben, III. *Revelation*. NCBC. New York: Cambridge University Press, 2003.

CPSIA information can be obtained
at www.ICGtesting.com
Printed in the USA
LVHW081958130919
630903LV00018B/10/P

9 781501 841743